Ten Secrets
of Successful Men
That Women Want to Know

Also by Dr. Donna Brooks and Lynn Brooks
Seven Secrets of Successful Women

Ten Secrets of Successful Men That Women Want to Know

⌒♌⌒

Dr. Donna Brooks and Lynn Brooks

McGraw-Hill

New York   Chicago   San Francisco   Lisbon   London
Madrid   Mexico City   Milan   New Delhi   San Juan
Seoul   Singapore   Sydney   Toronto

Library of Congress Cataloging-in-Publication Data

Brooks, Donna L., 1955–
   Ten secrets of successful men that women want to know/by Donna Brooks and
Lynn Brooks.
      p.cm.
Includes index.
   ISBN 0-07-138517-7 (hardcover:alk. paper)
   1. Success in business.   2. Businessmen.   I. Brooks, Lynn, 1955–   II. Title.
   HF5386 .B8473 2002
   650.1—dc21

                                                              2002003844

McGraw-Hill
A Division of The McGraw-Hill Companies

1   2   3   4   5   6   7   8   9   0   DOC/DOC   0   9   8   7   6   5   4   3   2

ISBN 0-07-138517-7

This book was set in Minion by North Market Street Graphics.

Printed and bound by R. R. Donnelley & Sons Company.

McGraw-Hill books are available at special quantity discounts to use as premiums
and sales promotions, or for use in corporate training programs. For more information, please write to the Director of Special Sales, Professional Publishing,
McGraw-Hill, Two Penn Plaza, New York, NY 10121-2298. Or contact your local
bookstore.

 This book is printed on recycled, acid-free paper containing a minimum
of 50% recycled, de-inked fiber.

Contents

Introduction

༓

Networks, mentors, and organizational initiatives level the playing field. This lets you in; it doesn't guarantee your personal success. The rest is up to you. It's like getting into the major leagues. You're a young baseball player with talent— you're in the minors; you've gotten into the game. Now what do you do? What's going to get you noticed so that you can play in the majors? Performance, skill, drive, making sure that others see your talent. . . . That's where women are today. You're in—now it's up to you to take charge of your career.

Did we get your attention with the title of this book? We meant to! We realize that different people may respond or react in different ways to this topic. Male readers probably picked up the book to see how they stack up—comparing their personal experiences with those of the men we interviewed—or to see what insights or strategies they can pick up. Period. They may coincidentally find that the senior female leaders interviewed in the book have had the same experiences, but I doubt that most men would have sought out their insights.

If you're a female reader, were you eager to read on to see what these "male" secrets of success are, something that goes on behind boardroom— or men's room—doors? Or perhaps you were outraged that we *appear* to be using a male model to gauge success? Let us assure you that we are most definitely not perpetuating a traditional male model that has existed for a century or more. On the contrary, we want to present a wide cross section of strategies and solutions that work in the real world—for both senior women and senior men. You'll read about many consistent strategies used by both the women and the men we interviewed. I believe that it's critical to have as much information as possible on how *everyone* in the workplace thinks, acts, and reacts so that we can stay on the cutting edge.

What we hear from our clients during our workshops are things like "I wish I had known these things ten years ago, earlier in my career. It took me forever to figure a lot of this stuff out on my own." So we asked our participants, "What skills really prepared you for your current position? Are there things you would have done differently? What advice would you give up-and-coming leaders? What about developing your personal style?" They gave us a lot of information on the career strategies that worked for them—and about what didn't work—and how they developed the skills that they use every day.

Who will benefit from these insights?

♦ Young women and men who are just starting their careers and are looking for good advice on career management

♦ Midcareer managers or aspiring managers who would like to fine-tune their skills and strategies

♦ Women who want to gain a better sense of the success strategies used by both senior women and men, strategies that provide a wider range of behaviors and attitudes

♦ Senior managers who would like a benchmark of what other leaders are doing to get ideas on different possible strategies for themselves and suggestions for skill building for their team members

I want to add that although most of the participants worked in corporations, their insights are highly valid in many environments. Lynn spent fifteen years in huge multinational corporations, while I spent ten years in higher education and then as an entrepreneur. In addition, in our research on women we have interviewed hundreds of women in corporations, higher education, the media, and politics. In all those situations the required skills were the same. In our research we found that different strategies work for different people at different times in different situations. You decide which ones may work for you.

WHY WE WROTE THIS BOOK

A few years ago Lynn and I wrote a book called *Seven Secrets of Successful Women,* in which we interviewed senior women to determine exactly how they became successful: Was it their skills, their strategies, their personalities, their environment, or their personal and professional experiences? We found, as you could probably guess, that it was a combination of all these factors. But what we also found through research instruments and in-depth interviews was that despite a number of underlying themes or strategies, there was no specific type or model of a "successful woman." Many of the women were warm and nurturing; some were more of a "tougher male model," if you want to call it that. Some were great communicators, others were experts in technology or finance, some prided themselves on their deliverables—getting the job done in a bottom-line fashion—and others valued their employees and developed a team attitude as their first priority.

We treated these characteristics as a bell curve, with traditional "male characteristics" at one end and "female characteristics" at the other end. (By the way, no, we do not believe that these categorizations of characteristics as male or female are necessarily accurate!) We have seen in our research that there are both women and men who score higher in the "female characteristics" while others are at the "masculine characteristics" end of the scale. What we found was that these traits or characteristics are based on gender *role* rather than on gender. We all know men who are warm and nurturing, great communicators and team builders—the "female characteristics" end of the gender scale. Likewise, we all know women who are decisive, analytical, logical, and bottom-line-oriented—more at the "male characteristics" end. Most of us are somewhere in the middle, combining various degrees of these characteristics.

What is most important about this finding is that we cannot assume that all women are at one end of the scale and all men are at the other end. Likewise, we cannot assume that women want to learn only the skills and strategies of other women. In fact, many—if not most—of the senior women we interviewed had male mentors or sponsors. In the last five years we have spoken to thousands of professional women (and men) in our presentations. Many women identify with men. Some women resist single-gender groups and prefer a more "real-world" mix of male and female colleagues. Others thoroughly enjoy groups of women in which they have the opportunity to share stories and experiences. Therefore, we have provided numerous opportunities to hear firsthand stories, strategies, and solutions from both male and female leaders in their fields.

THE RESEARCH

In this study we followed the same research strategy that we used in our last book: in-depth personal interviews, focus groups, and questionnaires, reflecting diversity in gender, race, culture, generation, and geographic location. It's important to note that we spoke with women *and* men—the key qualification was success, not gender. We asked participants questions about the skills and competencies that had helped them in their careers. What advice would you give to up-and-coming leaders, and what you would have done differently in your own career? What are some of the unique talents, skills, and values that women bring to the workplace? What areas may they need to develop? What areas do men need to develop? How do you motivate those who have not shown early leadership skills? What solutions to various leadership challenges or situations have you seen?

There was a clear theme to the responses, regardless of the methodology. First, when we examined the skills that leaders have found helpful in their careers—or the perception by others of what would be helpful to leaders—the following categories emerged:

- ◆ **Communication skills**—writing, interpersonal, listening, motivational

- ◆ **Personal style and image**—confident, good at "playing the game," focused, positive, detail-oriented, flexible, works well under pressure, determined, has endurance, analytical, performance-driven

- ◆ **Leadership: basic characteristics and competencies**—knowledgeable about work, intelligent, confident, focused, competent, prepared, can make tough decisions, tenacious, builds relationships and networks, mentors others, passionate

- ◆ **Leadership vision**—proactive (not reactive), innovative, creative, curious, visionary, able to motivate others

- ◆ **Team building**—identifying key skills needed in team members, keeping the team on target (why are we here?), communicating, setting goals, motivating, "taking care of your people"

In addition, we discussed perceptions of men and women at work. Overall, there were few, if any, surprises in the responses to questions such as, "What do women bring to organizations?" "What skills can they improve?" "What skills do men exhibit?" and "What do they need to work on?" It is important to note that although certain responses were more frequently cited by women or by men, there was a general agreement between men and women in their observations.

For example, an overwhelming number of the men indicated that women were outstanding in bringing people together, providing a different perspective in teams, communicating thoughtfully and clearly, and building relationships. Female participants cited the same strengths in themselves and other women. Likewise, women indicated that men are generally more decisive and assertive but need to be more inclusive, be better listeners, and practice not stepping on others to get what they want; the majority of men cited the same strengths and shortcomings.

The bottom line? Most of the participants agreed that there are few, if any, specific differences between men and women in *skill*. The differences that we will be discussing in the book refer more to differences in *style*. Both women and men know what the deal is: The challenge is to gain a greater understanding of the scope of the differences, rationalizing the extremes. You need to appreciate what works most effectively *for you* in a variety of situations: the skills, the behaviors, the leadership style.

With that in mind, you may be interested to see what the consensus seemed to be among our participants. *Keep in mind that these are often generalizations.* Below are some of the statements by men and women about their respective strengths and weaknesses. As I mentioned, for the most part there was considerable agreement with respect to their responses.

What do women excel at?

1. Organization, attention to detail, and keeping a focus on the goal
2. Consensus building, developing others, team building, compassion, empathy, nurturing
3. Networking and relationship building
4. Interpersonal relations, people skills, communication, listening, bringing a different perspective
5. Multitasking

What do women need to improve?

1. Assertiveness, toughness, and confidence—but without trying to be like men
2. Decision making
3. Visibility, marketing themselves, profile building, schmoozing
4. Negotiation, bargaining skills
5. Reactions to bargaining: taking things less personally, reacting less emotionally, accepting feedback, not being afraid to not be liked, working together better as women

What do men excel at?

1. Making decisions, acting decisively, getting the job done, concentrating on the bottom line
2. Speaking up: being assertive and confident, saying what's on one's mind, appearing commanding, intimidating others, getting to the point
3. Visibility: building a profile, making their presence known, being political, using "maleness" to get what they want
4. Delegating
5. Networking, moving upward socially, schmoozing

What do men need to improve?

1. Nurturing: acting with compassion, being more sensitive and less arrogant
2. Communicating: listening, offering feedback, clarifying instructions when necessary
3. Working as a team, sharing the spotlight, incorporating more inclusion and less posturing
4. Building relationships with female colleagues as well as with male colleagues
5. Not stereotyping female executives and other women at work

WHY DO WOMEN NEED A BOOK LIKE THIS IN THE TWENTY-FIRST CENTURY?

The perception of women by senior men in our research was extremely positive. In fact, not just positive—I was overwhelmed by how supportive and complimentary they were. These successful men—as well as their female counterparts—believe that women bring an incredible richness to organizations. They say that women motivate their teams better. In negotiations and conflict resolution women are willing to dig deeper to find a viable solution, and they encourage employees to have a life outside of work. They listen more carefully and give pertinent feedback, and they bring a different perspective to organizational issues. A large number of these leaders said that their female colleagues were extremely valued and respected in their organizations. As a result, although there are certainly exceptions, I believe that senior management in most organizations is often not the problem.

However, we have been hearing from our corporate clients that despite initiatives, networks, mentoring opportunities, and women in the pipeline, many women still aren't at the level that those organizations would have predicted or desired. Why not? Our opinion is that there is still a perception about women at work—one that is generally not accurate but is there nonetheless. There are still undertones among some employees that women often don't take work as seriously as men do, that they don't set career goals and pursue them as tenaciously as men do. Their families are often their primary concern, not their performance at work. Is this true? Perhaps in some cases it is, but probably not in most. Remember the bell curve of gender roles: Not all women are the same, nor are all men. Are there men in the workplace who don't set clear career goals or who choose to spend more time with their families at the expense of a fast-track career? Sure; I know quite a few myself. But somehow it seems to be more of a stigma for women.

In addition, there are little things that women *know* they need to do, such as increasing their visibility and developing more effective networks, but they may not know *how* to do it. Or they are still experimenting with their personal style and learning the right balance.

One of the questions we frequently get from women is: "Why do women have to change? Men know that they need to change their communication style and listen more effectively or be more inclusive, but they're not doing it. Why do we? It's not fair." You're right, it's not fair. Why do we have to change? Well, first of all, I always tell women: Don't change—simply learn to *adapt* to the situation or environment. Women bring an incredible richness to organizations, and most senior men and women agree. Read on for lots of examples.

Second, most senior men truly don't see differences in ability between men and women. They agree that women's styles sometimes differ, but that doesn't mean that they want these women to change. Many successful women add that they haven't wanted to—or had to—change. Their bosses and colleagues respect their perspective. Many senior men we interviewed stated that they look for—and find—the same skills and competencies in women as in men: being results-oriented, getting the job done, showing a talent for leadership, and so on. But women, they say, offer a different viewpoint or a different set of experiences, bringing a new perspective. Successful men and women have a common trait: outstanding performance. It's hard to argue with results. Even if others don't like your style, if you perform and deliver outstanding results, they're likely to get over the differences.

Lastly, although this is not a popular observation with some women, like it or not, many, if not most, organizations are still managed by men.

There has not been a great impetus for most men to change: Why should they? For many, things have been just fine the way they are and have been for generations. However, this *is* noticeably changing.

In my opinion—and many others have concurred—there are three reasons for the change:

1. **Organizations have no choice.** Many of the senior leaders we interviewed said that everyone is desperate for outstanding leaders and managers. There just aren't enough around. Thus, leaders are looking for skills and performance, not necessarily the perpetuation of an old boys' club.

2. **Senior men frequently have daughters, wives, and female friends who are in the workplace and are experiencing these outdated attitudes.** These fathers, husbands, and friends now tend to look at things from a new perspective, thanks to a female perspective at home.

3. **The problem is not usually at the highest levels of the corporation.** It's not as likely for the very senior men to be resistant to change. Most, if not all, of the men we interviewed were extremely egalitarian and proactive about encouraging women in their organizations. Many specifically mentioned that they did not see any differences in ability or skills between men and women. Instead, many women have said that the issue is more frequently with lower-level or midlevel managers. Perhaps they are insecure about having to compete with women for more senior positions, or maybe they're just jerks. (By the way, it's not just men we're talking about here. Plenty of women are guilty of this as well.) But slowly, the culture is changing.

WHAT DO WE DO ABOUT IT?

First, be proactive. Take a step back and evaluate your skills, behaviors, and style. Are they really where they need to be? Don't be defensive or make excuses. Look at the women and men who are successful. Are you like them? It's easy to say, "Well, they don't have kids," "They have a boss who helps them," "They have the right personality," or "They toot their own horn." You may not like them, but make a conscious effort to analyze why they are successful. This can take time and it's not easy, but it has to be done. Is there a pattern among these successful people? Do they all seem to have the same skills, personality, and style? I bet you'll find that they don't. But I bet that they perform and get results—or at least they convince others that they work hard and perform.

Then you have to decide: Can I adapt or change? Do I want to change? Should I be in a different department? Do I need to develop my existing skills or learn new ones by going back to school? Should I change my image or find an advocate within the company? These are the basic questions you need to ask. Then you go to the next level.

Okay, you know that you need outstanding skills. Now do whatever you need to do not only to get them up to par but to exceed expectations. Look for new opportunities, take on jobs no one else wants—and do a great job! Overprepare for every meeting; know more than you have to. Don't just do your "assignment" or work only within your job description. Work a bit harder and take projects to the next step; don't just complete what you have been asked to do.

What about your boss? Is he or she helping you develop your skills, visibility, and leadership opportunities? If not, communicate with your boss: Is he or she knowingly holding you back or just unaware that he or she is not helping you? Work on your network, and if your manager is holding you back, find out about other opportunities, other projects, other departments, even other companies or industries. Go out and find a number of mentors, coaches, advocates, supporters, and sponsors and ask them for advice and direction. Take—or make—opportunities to be visible. Take a few risks, but ask your mentor or advocate about the pros and cons.

Be aware that there are still perceptions by men (and even by other women) that many women need to be tougher, more decisive, and more assertive. (But not too assertive—there's a fine line! A number of our participants advised women "not to try too hard to be like men; it usually doesn't work.") Also, many women admit that they still have difficulty gaining visibility: It doesn't come naturally to them, or they need to network more, or they don't have mentors, advocates, or sponsors and don't know how to get them.

It can be overwhelming, but you can learn the best strategies from both the men and the women we interviewed and adapt them to your own environment.

Listen to what these women and men are saying in our questionnaires and interviews.

♦ What do they really think?

♦ What are some suggestions, strategies, and solutions we heard in our interviews?

♦ What have these leaders done that might work for you?

♦ Do you recognize yourself in some of these scenarios and stories?

- Do you need to find a number of advocates, mentors, or sponsors?
- Do you need to improve your visibility?
- Do you want to work on your image or personal style? Do you need to change it? How?
- Do you need to improve your team-building skills, presentation skills, or financial skills?
- Do you need to go back to school or get more training?
- Do you need to develop content expertise and let everyone know what it is?

Our participants consistently talked about the skills and competencies that helped them become successful regardless of industry or experience. From their insights we have identified ten major themes, or secrets of success:

1. Develop your personal brand.
2. Create an image and a style that work for you.
3. Define your role as a team leader or team participant.
4. Develop a mentoring network.
5. Build effective networks.
6. Gain global experience and insights.
7. Take charge of your own career.
8. Develop winning communication skills.
9. Develop key leadership skills.
10. Develop the next generation of leaders.

These strategies can work for you. Listen to these experts—both men and women—and find out how.

Participants

We would like to extend our appreciation to the following executives who provided their views and insights on leadership:

- Joël Anik, Managing Partner, Andersen
- Malcolm Armstrong, Air Transport Association
- Willa Baynard, Vice President, JP Morgan Chase
- Joseph Berardino, Chief Executive Officer, Andersen
- Rand Blazer, Chief Executive Officer, KPMG Consulting
- Klaus Bodel, Training Manager for Leadership Programs and Management Development, BMW
- Walt Boomer, Chief Executive Officer, Rogers Company
- Liz Brown, Partner, Management Consulting Services, PriceWaterhouse Coopers
- William Burns, former Chief U.S. Negotiator, Salt II Arms Reduction Treaty
- Jolie Caldwell
- Marshall Carter, Senior Fellow, Harvard University JFK School of Government/former Chief Executive Officer, State Street Financial
- Julian Childs, Former Executive Vice President/Chief Operating Officer, international financial information company
- Michael Clark, Executive Vice President, JP Morgan Chase
- Frank Cuttita, Chief Administrative Officer, Columbus Circle Investors

- Neil DeFeo, Chief Executive Officer, Remington Products
- Phil DeFeo, Chief Executive Officer, the Pacific Exchange
- Gary Dibb, Chief Administrative Officer, Barclays Bank
- Ronald Dykes, Chief Financial Officer, BellSouth Corporation
- John Everett, Senior Partner, Deloitte Consulting, United Kingdom
- Jim Foster, Chief Administrative Officer, Citigroup Europe
- David Fung, Regional General Manager, international financial news service
- Eric Gibson, Senior Director, Corporate Training and Development, Wyeth Ayerst Laboratories
- Richard Guenther, Vice President, Global Network Services, Unisys Corporation
- Patrick Harker, Dean of the Wharton School of the University of Pennsylvania
- Chuck Henry, President, LFR Group (subsidiary of FC International, Paris)
- John Joyce, Chief Financial Officer, IBM Corporation
- Nathan Kantor, President/Chief Operating Officer, Winstar Communications
- Christian Koffmann, Chairman, Consumer Products Worldwide, Johnson & Johnson
- Rick Lieb, Chief Executive Officer, SEI Investments
- Luiz Lima, Regional Director, Securities Services, Americas, Citigroup
- Vernon Loucks, Retired Chief Executive Officer, Baxter International
- Gena McCleary
- Patrick McLaurin, Senior Vice President, Diversity, Booz Allen Hamilton
- Steven Meadows, Executive Vice President/Managing Director, Citigroup Europe
- Denise Menelly, Director, Corporate and Investment Bank, Citigroup
- Ben Montoya, Interim CEO, SmartSystems Technologies
- Denis Nayden, Chairman and Chief Executive Officer, GE Capital
- Harry Pearce, Chairman, Hughes Electronics/Vice Chairman, General Motors

- Mike Robb, Executive Vice President, Real Estate Division, Pacific Life Insurance Company
- Phillip Rooney, Executive Vice President, ServiceMaster Management Services Group
- Glenn Schafer, President, Pacific Life Insurance Company
- James Schiro, Chief Executive Officer, PriceWaterhouse Coopers
- Carol Stuckley, Vice President Treasury, Pfizer
- Richard Thorne, Former Chief Operations Officer/Managing Director, wireless telecommunications industry, Netherlands/United Kingdom
- Tim Tyson, President, Worldwide Manufacturing/Supply Operations, Glaxo SmithKline
- Philip Vasan, Managing Director, Credit Suisse First Boston
- Joseph Vipperman
- Lawrence Weinbach, Chief Executive Officer, Unisys Corporation
- Alicia Whitaker, Managing Director, Credit Suisse First Boston
- Robert Wolf, Global Head of Fixed Income, UBS Warburg

In addition, we would like to thank all of our participants who chose to remain anonymous, as well as those from the following organizations who provided their valuable insights: American Express, DuPont, Johnson & Johnson, Marriott, Merck, Merrill Lynch, Pfizer, PriceWaterhouse Coopers, Rohm & Haas, Unisys, and Wyeth-Ayerst Laboratories.

Develop Your Personal Brand

Acquiring and Promoting Key Competencies and Skills

✧

The good news—and it is largely good news—is that every-one has a chance to stand out. Everyone has a chance to learn, improve, and build up their skills. Everyone has a chance to be a brand worthy of remark.[1]

A s we discussed in the introduction, performance is one of the most important themes of our research. As one executive at EDS says, "Being smart is the price of admission: What counts is how effective you are." We have been sharing this with our clients for years. It is important to have—and equally important to let others *know* you have—skills and competencies critical to your organization. One of the things we have heard, not only from our research participants but also in the press, is that there aren't enough good leaders out there. But one of the things I have realized is that there *are* frequently outstanding potential leaders out there who are not aware of their potential or have not been identified by those who undertake the task of leadership development. It is important to examine and highlight your skills and competencies and critically evaluate the gaps in order to advance your career—and then let others know what you can do.

DEVELOPING KEY COMPETENCIES AND SKILLS

In many of our training programs we ask the participants to identify some of the main skills and competencies that are important in their organizations, their functions, and their teams. Here is a short list of the kinds of skills and competencies they identify.

- Results-driven communication: one on one and in teams
- Presentation and speaking skills
- Strong financial skills
- Knowledge of a broad spectrum of issues, even outside one's current area or in other departments: technology, international
- Flexibility and adaptability
- Strategic thinking; thinking outside the box
- Technical skills
- Comfort level in decision making
- Going beyond observations and reports to one's boss—analyzing, integrating, projecting, recommending
- Outstanding negotiation skills
- Comfort with risks
- Ability to manage teams
- Ability to persuade

Many of our participants also suggest developing content expertise. Identify your expertise in a certain area or identify key competencies that will distinguish you on your team or in your department. You're the person people turn to with questions. Here is what several had to say:

You don't necessarily have to excel at a number of skills. Even just one area of expertise is adequate. But even if you only have one good skill, make sure that you develop it to its fullest extent. And let others know that you have this skill—don't assume that others know about it.

∞

I'm known for my deliverables: If I say I'm going to get something done, it gets done. I often get the tough jobs, the jobs other people don't want, because I've had good success in these situations. When it comes down to it, the company is looking for results.

∞

Of critical importance in my career has been developing a deep level of competence in my chosen area of practice as well as a deep understanding of my clients' business and the challenges they face. I make a commitment to do the best work possible for my clients, and honoring that commitment would be difficult—if not impossible—without the necessary skills and business knowledge.

My company brought me in because it needed someone with broad-based experience. In my last job I did everything: finance, operations, technology, accounting. I felt confident that even though it was a different environment, I had very transferable skills.

Lynn also found that it was helpful to write extremely comprehensive market reports for her organization, since she was responsible for international marketing, specifically in Latin America and Asia. She wrote those reports regularly, reflecting various market conditions and current political, economic, and social issues and how they had affected or could affect the company's sales in those regions. Not only did it keep her up to speed on what was going on in her markets, it provided essential data so that her company could make timely decisions that were based on accurate data rather than having to wait for the information. However, once she had created a template with specific topics, it was relatively easy to input the data and make an analysis. She didn't have to reinvent the wheel. As a by-product, she was also known as the content expert on these areas and established credibility in this area.

It's a great idea to distribute these reports to colleagues, your boss, the executive committee, the senior management team, and key players, depending on your particular situation. Of course, let your boss in on the plan, don't keep her or him out of the loop. (Bosses don't like surprises. There's nothing worse than having your boss find out what you're doing from someone above her or him.)

Integrate various aspects of analysis, synthesize them, and create informative reports from a macro/micro perspective—the specifics as well as the big picture. Make yourself indispensable to the organization. Develop expertise in the following areas:

♦ Market environment: outlook and projections (what's going on in your industry as well as outside that can affect your industry)

♦ Strategic competitive analysis (what your competitors are doing)

Make Yourself the Content Expert: Create an Individual Action Plan

♦ What are your areas of expertise? What are you known for? What do people come to you for information on?

♦ If you don't have one, what area or areas should you develop? How?

- What skills/competencies are valued at your organization/in your department/on your team?
- You may want to distribute reports or updates on
  —Research you have done on your content area or other areas
  —Competitive strategic analysis
  —Ways to increase productivity within the organization
  —Ways to develop new markets
- How will you accomplish this (formally, informally, individual, group)?
- Who should receive this information?
  —Your boss and colleagues
  —The executive committee
  —The senior management team
  —Other key players
  —Outside entities

One of our participants added an interesting perspective on the importance of developing an area of expertise, particularly for women:

I would suggest they focus sooner. The move from generalist to specialist is one that most women and minorities have trouble making. The problem is that women and minorities often have a strong set of skills across a spectrum of disciplines: That allows them to have success early in their careers in almost any setting in which they find themselves. But this generalist competence will take you only so far. You will find that your career is a continual series of midlevel roles in which you work very hard, are spread all over the place, but never seem to get the big promotion that takes you off the midlevel management merry-go-round.

When I have examined this, the usual crisis is the belief "But to focus on one thing means I have to close all the other doors." To some extent this is true, and I know I experienced it myself. I think women and minorities usually feel insecure in their roles, and by keeping a broad set of skills and interests active, we keep our options open and also seem to add more value to the organization.

But the fact is that it doesn't add more value to your career. The reality is that it is okay to close some doors. To have a deep, functional knowledge and expertise in a given area, you almost have to focus on that to the exclusion of other interests. As you gain this deep expertise, you become more and more the expert in an area. At this point you will be able to add greater value to the firm and also to your own career. Once you start gaining stature in the organization and move up, you can start to broaden your range of interests again and get involved in other areas.

I have heard this referred to as the "hourglass" model, in which, ideally, a person has a breadth of experience early in his or her career (the large bottom of the hourglass), then focuses and becomes very narrowly defined (the middle stem of the hourglass), and then again broadens his or her perspective later (the large top part of the hourglass). No matter the model, women and minorities often stay in the "breadth" mode longer than they should or need to.

Another participant agreed:

My career covered a number of different content areas: operations, financial control, treasury/risk. While it has been wonderful experience, in retrospect, I probably should have invested more time in fewer different content areas.

As you read these quotes, keep in mind that gaining content expertise and developing broad-based knowledge are not mutually exclusive. Leaders need to have broad-based knowledge and experience as part of their tool kit, but at different times in their careers they need to focus on using only several of the tools. The experience and knowledge are still there. As our participant added, "Once you start gaining stature in the organization and move up, you can start to broaden your range of interests again and get involved in other areas."

Create Your Personal "Tool Kit"

Proactively evaluate your career. Ask yourself the tough questions. For example, are there areas in your experience or skill set that you may need to update? We have heard several people call this a personal "tool box." It's an excellent analogy. Think about it: Every specialist has a set of tools required for the job. Surgeons have their surgical instruments; plumbers, carpenters, and electricians have their tools of the trade. What tools do you need for your job? This will be specific to your environment, and you may have to add tools to the box. When you begin a job in technology, for example, it will include, of course, technical content expertise. But as you move up, you may manage a team, for which you will also need team leadership and communication skills. Many people will then need presentation skills as they increasingly interact on a higher level with other departments or when they present a project update to senior management. You can see the importance of identifying which skills you will need in the future—not only the basic ones you need now. And you need to start working on this now!

How do you know which skills you'll need? Certainly, talk to your boss or colleagues in your field. Talk to them about what they do, what they needed to develop, and how they did it. Talk to mentors, advocates, and others about what they see on a larger scale, not necessarily just your next position. Many skills and competencies are easily transferable to other departments.

One colleague, a director at a major pharmaceutical firm, had a degree in engineering and had worked in computer science for twenty years. However, a highly visible pilot program position became available under human resources for which her boss and mentor recommended her. He was able to see her potential outside of her job description and knew that she had developed the essential skills to do a great job (which, of course, she did). Ironically, she hadn't specifically prepared her tool kit for this position, but it was something that she naturally had an affinity and passion for. You never know.

One of the other things that we have heard is that some executives have identified their gaps as a result of assessing their skill sets—and have done some interesting things to round out those sets. Some of those things are not necessarily what you might expect. One senior executive found that after receiving a liberal arts degree, he needed to go back to get solid business credentials.

Part of a good education is improving your business qualifications with studies of practical subjects. I augmented liberal arts studies at Cambridge with an accountancy certification. I realized the importance of understanding numbers to the extent that I could consequently make sound business decisions.

Another executive received a degree in economics and statistics, but even with this business background, he found that a certification in accountancy was needed to round out his credentials.

In a different direction, one CEO with a background in finance has developed an interest in things such as classic literature, which he feels has greatly enhanced his understanding and appreciation of philosophy and history, especially as they relate to the modern world. Another participant, a general, added that his liberal arts education was one of his most valuable assets, allowing him to "set a standard or foundation" on which all his later decisions could be based. As we mentioned several times in the research, having broad-based experience is a key element of leadership success.

I credit my "leadership skill set" for my own success, which includes, I believe, my ability to inspire trust and loyalty among my staff, being a good listener, as well as being a "quick study"—being decisive and willing to take on new challenges. I've always raised my hand when someone was looking for a volunteer to go where there was a problem. Were I to do it all over again, though, I would have gone for earlier experience in sales and marketing to get a broader base of experience.

⌗

I've always considered people skills extremely important for a leader. This isn't something I learned at the university—I learned it growing up at home with my family. When you've gone through tough issues at home, you tend not to be so detached: You understand what your staff might be going through.

Several top leaders credit their experience in and comfort with working with numbers as a factor in their success.

If I had to offer any leadership advice to women, it would be to get more experience with numbers. Having studied engineering, I had a "tool box" when I started my career. I felt comfortable with numbers and when discussing issues in a quantitative fashion. I believe that many women don't come to their careers with that same comfort level. My university class, for example, was less than 10 percent women. I see that some women don't like doing budgets, and this limits their advancement. Although this trend is starting to change, it's something to be aware of.

⌗

I've always been curious, analytical. I love numbers. In Brazil there are a number of different issues to deal with: inflation, instability. My background proved particularly helpful in that environment, versus the typical issues that you might face in the United States.

In addition, a solid academic background and a current résumé detailing your education and skills are always good tools to have on hand.

A good academic background is so important. I've seen a number of people fail in midcareer because of a lack of a solid education. And of course, global awareness is key to becoming a strong leader.

⌗

For people who are three to five-plus years into their career, I ask, "Do you have a current résumé?" Usually, it's one to three years old. "Have you prepared a skills and experience matrix?" This is a catalogue of skills: functional skills, job experience, and so forth. "Have you ever prepared a budget? Have you ever worked in sales, marketing, or advertising? Have you ever had any direct reports? Have your direct reports had their own direct reports (have you managed several layers?)? Have you ever developed MBOs?" You should have a career plan for the next three to five years. Set objectives. It may require a couple of lateral moves to reach that objective—you need to recognize that.

In addition to creating a tool kit of skills, Tom Peters recommends asking yourself several questions to define who you are—your personal brand. First, identify "the qualities and characteristics that make you distinctive from your competitors—or your colleagues. What have you done lately to make yourself stand out? What would your colleagues or your customers say is your greatest and clearest strength or your most noteworthy personal trait? What do you do that adds value? Do you deliver your work on time, every time? Do you anticipate problems before they become crises? What do you do that adds measurable value? What do you do that you are most proud of?"

He suggests several options for increasing your skill level—and gaining visibility. Try signing up for an extra project to introduce yourself to colleagues and showcase your skills—or learn new ones. Do an external project, event, or volunteer opportunity. Teach a class internally or externally. Write an article or opinion piece in your newspaper or professional publication. Participate in a panel discussion or workshop. Build your reputation on the basis of your content knowledge and expertise. Have people think of you first when assigning projects. Keep on top of your skills: Are they still on target based on your organization's needs? What's your value today—and tomorrow?[2]

Put some effort into finding out how the pipelines work. For example, in banking, credit training is necessary for advancement. You need to develop key skills for this, or a number of jobs get closed off to you. Often it was perceived that only "geeky guys" go into credit training, a decision which is generally made early in one's career. You have to ask yourself, "What are the core competencies? How have I prepared myself for mastery of those skills?" People may be comfortable in human resources or public relations, etc., in the lower ranks, but that can hold you back later in your career in my organization. Credit training and risk management are central to many positions; they are essential in a large number of top jobs. There are many more senior choices later. Human relations and communications, for example, only have one top job. It's like a pyramid.

LETTING OTHERS KNOW ABOUT YOUR ACCOMPLISHMENTS—SUBTLY

I'm going to be blatantly sexist here: I believe that men have perfected the art of posturing and bragging about their accomplishments and made it an art form. They're better at this than women. There, I've said it. Well, of course, this was one of the major responses in our questionnaire when we asked, "What do men do well?" But all kidding aside, there are many effective ways to promote yourself and your talents. Many women admit that they don't feel comfortable calling attention to their skills, and this can lead others to believe that they aren't as competent as they really are.

In addition to talent and skill, it's important to be perceived as competent as well. Gain early successes in projects or on teams—and let others know about them. If you're not comfortable tooting your own horn, make sure someone else gets the word out for you—and don't leave this to chance.

∽

Women don't seem to have as much confidence in themselves as others—including their bosses—have in them. It's okay not to feel 100 percent sure of your ability, but showing confidence is different from being aggressive.

I was watching a program on British Special Forces training on the Discovery Channel recently. (Yes, I practice what I preach—broad-based interests and knowledge.) A British commando, having finished his mountain training—after an incredibly grueling six-month training program that probably 99.9 percent of the population could never do—took part in the final two-day military exercise and mock battle, which would determine whether the participants would pass or fail the entire program. (Of course, he passed with flying colors.) After he successfully completed the exercise, I was amused by his comment (keep in mind that the British are known for their hesitation to call attention to themselves). He said, "Well, no one likes to blow their own trumpet, but I did do well in the exercises." That about sums it up for me. Performance speaks volumes. I loved the understatement, and I thought that it was a good example of subtly calling attention to one's accomplishments.

A little closer to home, a few years ago I was leading a team to interview a young guy, a few years out of college, who was not our leading candidate. But he was great at self-promotion. When we asked him about his experience in leading teams, he said, "Well, I put together a big marketing event, and, well, my boss said it was the biggest success we had ever had. Everyone said it was a huge success." Notice how he deflected the flattery—"My boss said. . . ." Keep that one in mind for the future—it's a keeper.

Do you ever notice that some men *seem* to know a lot about a lot of things—except *you* happen to know that they don't? It's the perception of competence again. Many men have learned that it's important to seem competent and skilled at a young age. When my older brother was about sixteen or seventeen, for example, he applied for a summer construction job in order to make money to buy a new sports car. These kinds of jobs paid a lot more money than most others did. When the boss asked him, "Can you drive a truck?" He said, "Sure, no problem." Well, of course he had never driven a truck before. He just figured that he would learn what he needed to know as he went along. He got the job, and of course he did fine.

So how can we promote ourselves subtly and seem confident when we're doing it? Literally, as I was writing this sentence, a friend of mine called and said that she heard about a job opening that she wanted to pursue. She is incredibly successful and outgoing, has unbelievable credentials, and is a good friend of the person who will be hiring for this position. I said, "Hey, just give him a call tomorrow and get together for lunch. You always have a great time talking to him anyway." She said, "I know, but it's really weird. Sometimes I just get a little shy about doing things like that. I guess I feel like I'm putting them out or something." I told her that I was writing about this topic "as we speak" and gave her a few examples of other successful women who feel the same way. "Oh, what the heck," she said. "I'll take him to lunch, and if nothing else we'll have a great chance to catch up." The lesson here? Sometimes you need someone to provide a different perspective and encourage you to subtly toot your own horn. Look to your support network. I've done the same thing for many people—and they have done it for me. Sounds simple—and it is!

If you still feel uncomfortable, go to plan B. Let another person be your advocate. If appropriate, arrange for someone in your support network to "talk you up" to someone else. You know that you will be able to return the favor in the future. Most people have no problem promoting someone else. Especially if you have a great relationship with that person, he or she is usually happy to do it. Don't hesitate to ask. These people can tout your accomplishments casually.

You can also submit information to your organizational newsletter, internal e-mail, or corporate communications: They're always looking for positive information of interest. I happened to notice a particularly interesting example of this while I was visiting the Ernst and Young Web site. A young consultant, Genevieve Brame, was prominently featured on the home page of her company's site in the "People" section, complete with a photograph. She had recently published a book on living and working in France, sponsored by her company, the French Ministry of Foreign Affairs, and the *International Herald Tribune*. I thought, Wow, what a great way to create visibility not only for your firm internationally but also for yourself. Find out if your organization has such a section on its Web site and how you can publicize your accomplishments.

You may even want to submit a story to the local newspaper if you are working on a volunteer project or another event of interest, particularly if it is business related and reflects well on your organization. Don't assume that other people know who you are and what you do—they don't! And if you have something published or highlighted in the media, let others know about it. A good way? Show it to someone with whom you have a great relationship. That person will be excited for you and make a copy and pass it around. Look for subtle opportunities to let others know what you can do.

Sometimes you never know where you may be visible, and so it's a good idea to always be prepared to shine. When I was recently talking to one of my clients, a senior executive, about doing a program on networking, we were assessing the logistics and format of various exercises. We decided on tables of about eight to ten people who would discuss several questions on work-related topics. A senior manager would be seated at each table to help the flow, keep the participants on track, and report the results of the discussion. Pretty standard stuff. However, what I found fascinating is that she happened to mention that when she is at a company or industry function such as this, she always likes to take the opportunity to spot new talent. She commented:

I love having roundtable discussions at internal programs or seminars which are based on a case study, question, or organizational challenge. Not only do the participants have an opportunity to share their ideas, challenges, and solutions, but I get to sit back and observe. I'm always on the lookout for new talent and good ideas, and it's a great opportunity for me to see how people act, interact, think, and come up with good solutions to problems.

We hadn't even been talking about visibility—it was just about a program on networking. But her statement concurs with what we have told many women and men: Never miss an opportunity to make an impression. Think hard the next time you're in any kind of gathering. There very well may be someone who is assessing you on how you act or react in any kind of situation. Are you going to be someone who that person will remember? Did you say something that impressed him or her? What kind of image did you convey?

Several of our participants shared their observations.

I was at a company meeting in which we had to work in teams, small groups, and then present our observations and suggestions. One young woman gave her team presentation and, unknown to her, the president of the company was in the audience. He was so impressed with her poise and delivery that he specifically requested that she be put on the "fast track" via a highly visible position and more challenging opportunities.

౷

I was at an industry event with a cocktail reception at the end and started chatting with the CEO of a major corporation. Six months later, when a highly visible position became available at his organization, he specifically requested that I be put on the "short list" for the position. I got the job.

౷

Find new ways of doing things. Don't just talk about an idea at a meeting; spend some time and energy presenting a completed project idea. Find something that's never been done, read industry information outside your area, and learn about the whole company, not just your area.

Create a Professional Portfolio

A way to subtly highlight your accomplishments in a different manner is to create a professional portfolio. More than a résumé, it includes all kinds of details on who you are. What are you especially proud of? That's usually not on your résumé or application. What makes you stand out? What are the things that you usually don't think to tell other people but that are an integral part of who you are?

There are a few different ways that you can design this portfolio, depending on your needs and environment. First, it can be just a sheet of paper with all kinds of interesting information, perhaps in bullet form—a personal information sheet. I use one, for example, when my clients want to know more about what I do in addition to the standard brochures with company information. Mine has information on my background, my research, media write-ups, international experience, languages I speak, even things like "I've completely renovated three houses." It gives a broader picture of who you are.

Another approach is to do an actual portfolio, a packet of information. You could include samples of your work, letters of commendation, awards you have won, marketing pieces you have produced, and technical manuals you have created. It can contain anything you want people to know about you. It gives so much more than a résumé ever could.

When can you use this portfolio? A lot of our clients love the idea for the annual review process. It allows employees to gather information and share it with the boss or others to underscore what they accomplished that year, not only at work but with volunteerism, high-level sports or academic accomplishments, and other nonwork activities. It helps the employee focus on what he or she has done this year.

Other applications could include interviews. A one-page "cheat sheet" with bullet points not only can help the interviewers focus on your various accomplishments, but you can pass it out subtly to the interviewers and keep one in front of you for reference. It takes a lot of the anxiety out of the interview—thinking that you're going to forget to mention something of importance. You can also present it to a potential mentor to give that person a quick background, in an information interview, as background information when someone wants a bio on you, or to your new boss, who may not know you and has never seen your résumé (which is probably out of date anyway).

Below is a list of some of the things you could include, but use your imagination. When you are developing your list, I would suggest that you do it with one or two close colleagues or friends. Not only can you enjoy the chance to get together and have fun, you will encourage more creativity—others see you differently than you see yourself. What you may consider average or routine and wouldn't think to add is probably outstanding to others.

Here are some of the things that you can include, among many others:

♦ Academic and/or sports accomplishments
♦ Interesting or unique skills, personal or professional
♦ Technical and software proficiencies
♦ Seminars and conferences conducted or attended

- Workshop and keynote speaking
- Outstanding sales results
- Membership or leadership in volunteer organizations
- Civic association membership or leadership
- Political campaigns
- Grants written and obtained, funding obtained
- Research papers, proposals, or projects
- Media opportunities
- Foreign exchange opportunities (host or participant)
- Articles or books written
- Web sites created
- Press releases
- Technical or other manuals written or produced
- Training programs completed or conducted
- Promotional materials produced
- Letters of commendation

Add Value to the Organization—Showcase Your Skills

Sometimes you have a great idea to add value that the organization hasn't thought about yet. There's probably a good way to pursue what you see as a great idea—and a less effective way. First, a good idea of what *not* to do.

Many years ago when I was a college administrator, I made the mistake of not having a good plan for what I thought was a great idea to add value to my organization. Since my background was largely international, I thought that our college should have a comprehensive international program of foreign study for the students and exchange opportunities for the professors. I did tons of research on what similar colleges were doing, called colleagues, did a lot of work on my own time, and presented a proposal . . . but none of the senior decision makers could have cared less about an international program. It wasn't in their strategic plan; they didn't see the value. I was disappointed—and somewhat annoyed that they were so parochial as to fail to see the great value such a program would provide. Why didn't they think it was a great idea? What had I done wrong?

Well, first, I didn't get the buy-in from several key decision makers. I assumed that everyone would love it as much as I did. In addition, I didn't have a more senior sponsor pushing for me, bringing up my project at senior meetings, and giving me credibility. It just didn't get on anyone's radar. If I had to do it over again,

- ◆ I would talk to key people to see how they felt about such a program.
- ◆ I would sell key people on the idea individually and get them excited.
- ◆ I would seek a sponsor—someone who could give me advice, give me credibility, get the topic discussed at senior meetings, and "talk it up."
- ◆ I would collect lots of data to quantify my proposal: statistics from other colleges, including
  1. Their return on investment from the international programs
  2. Measurable results, such as a certain percentage increase in enrollment resulting from having such a program
  3. Increase in satisfaction at the college because of the international program, based on surveys of students and faculty members
  4. Improved perception by students and depth of knowledge of their faculty
  5. Increased ability by faculty and students to think more globally

Measurements matter. Business is run (mostly) by numbers. So, if you can make your case with statistics, it will get a better hearing.[3]

Well, live and learn. Here's an example of a *successful* presentation of an innovative idea. One senior executive recalls a success story involving one of his employees:

Ten years ago service was an afterthought in our industry—it was more marketing than customer service. A young employee, a self-starter, came to me with an idea that had not yet been explored—no other insurance companies had ever done it before. An MBA from the University of Chicago, he came to me with a plan: He wanted terminals with imaged documents for all customer service people so that those employees could talk to customers with actual documents and information in front of them to enhance service. I thought it was a great idea, but I had to run blocker for him a number of times—the idea was not immediately embraced.

In 1994, before this concept, we were 105th in sales. By 1997, our sales had skyrocketed and our industry had voted us "Best Service in the U.S.," a distinction we still hold. Without him, we wouldn't have had this success. Now, ten years later, this young manager has become senior vice president of strategic planning, based largely on his ability to identify and integrate new concepts. He has had a key impact on both the company and the industry.

You can increase your potential for visibility and success by identifying a novel new idea, presenting a detailed big-picture plan, and gaining support from a sponsor who can "talk up your idea" and give it legitimacy.

Tips on Increasing Your Visibility

1. **Become more involved in teams, projects, and committees.** Don't hesitate to ask to be assigned to high-visibility teams or projects. Let your boss or others know that you're interested. They can't read your mind.

2. **Get involved in volunteer opportunities at work and outside of work:** charities, holiday events, walkathons. You'll meet people you usually don't have the opportunity to meet.

3. **Become a good researcher.** Use the Internet, personal sources of information, and pertinent publications in your field (newspapers, magazines, online info). Copy interesting articles or other information of interest to team members and/or senior management. Distribute informational reports to your boss, other managers, key players, and the like. Be able to discuss the latest developments in your field with your bosses and colleagues.

4. **Observe the style of teams, groups, or meetings.** Depending on the style, you may have to jump in when you have something to say. Often you can't "wait your turn" to be heard. It probably won't come! But make sure that you have something worth saying. If you make a statement promising or proposing something, make sure you can back it up with numbers or statistics. Be prepared—know more than you need to know.

5. **Ask to job shadow a more senior manager.** If it doesn't concern sensitive or confidential material, ask to attend meetings that can help you learn more about the company or a new project.

6. **Examine ways in which you can add value to your organization:** increasing sales revenues, saving money in the department, increasing productivity. Talk to advocates and/or mentors about your ideas and see if they are congruent with the organization.

7. **Develop a clear skill set:** a content expertise. What are you known for? What do others come to you for? Are you a technical expert? Are you good at "fixing" an organization or team? Are you an outstanding project manager? Are you known for "deliverables" (if you say you're going to do something, does the rest of your team consider it done?)? Do you have international experience? Let everyone know what you can do—constantly and consistently. Don't assume they already know.

8. **Make sure potential mentors think about you periodically.** Keep them updated on your activities, achievements, and projects. Ask your mentor or advocate for advice and feedback on your plan to gain visibility.

9. **Ask senior managers for advice:** which professional and other organizations to join as well as which resources, journals, and periodicals to be familiar with. Ask your boss or other managers to get together for an informal lunch, either alone or with others, depending on your comfort level and style.

10. **Validate your employees' or colleagues' statements when you speak in meetings:** "Mary brings up an interesting point." "I agree 100 percent with John's statement." Or ask trusted colleagues to validate yours.

11. **Submit personal and departmental/team accomplishments to corporate communications/the public relations department for distribution.** Also, submit them to local or national media, as appropriate.

12. **Take a course on presentation skills or join Toastmasters to augment your speaking or presentation skills.** Take the opportunity to examine and update your technical, presentation, and other appropriate skills. Let others know.

13. **See who's getting noticed and moving ahead.** Pay careful attention to the senior people to imitate the way they dress, speak, treat others, and handle situations. Many senior women and men advise that you listen to those who are being heard:
    - How do they speak?
    - What is their body language?
    - Where can you learn the language and/or buzzwords of your area or an area you're interested in?

SUMMARY

Success Secret #1: Develop Your Personal Brand: Acquiring and Promoting Key Competencies and Skills

1. Review your skill set and create your tool box. What do you need to develop, to add? How will you let others know about your skills and competencies?

2. Focus on continually improving your performance. Performance is an important theme among our participants: performance on projects, on teams, on delivering results, and on doing what you say you'll do.

3. Review and publicize your skills. What do you bring to the table? Do you know what your organization's competitors are doing? Do you have a track record of increasing sales? Have you had great success at negotiation? Do you get projects done on time and on budget?

4. Make yourself a content expert. Create an individual action plan.

5. In your career, move from "generalist" to "specialist" and then broaden your range again.

6. Let others know, directly or subtly, what you can do—your accomplishments.

7. Take advantage of every situation to stand out, from small-group training exercises to team projects.

8. Create a professional portfolio; it helps you identify skills—and gaps. It can also help in your performance reviews.

9. If you are looking to start an initiative, be sure to get organizational buy-in and support. Make sure that it is congruent with organizational goals.

For a list of research participants, please see page xvii.

Create an Image and a Style
That Work for You

ぐ\ふ

Leadership is a performance. You have to be conscious of your behavior, because everyone else is. Leaders spend a lot of time making sure they come across with the right message in the way they walk, talk, dress, and stand. It's not only action, it's also about acting.

Leaders deliver. Before, ideas and being cool have counted. What counts now? Performance. Results.[1]

W hile discussing employee bonuses during a partners meeting, one senior executive noticed that it was interesting to see how each partner talked up his or her own team members to maximize the employees' bonuses. "What struck me was that each partner seemed to focus on the skills or competencies he or she saw as valued at the firm," he said. The bottom line was that they seemed to reward people who were seen to perform. No surprise. "One guy said, for example, 'You should see this guy on my team; he works from 6 A.M. to 6 P.M. Then he's always sending e-mails from home; he really works hard.'" It was obvious in this organization that working hard (long hours) really mattered and was valued—and this employee knew how to get noticed. Maybe he really was an exceptionally hard worker who delivered results, or maybe he was just good at playing the game, but his *image* was that of a person who was "really hardworking."

WHAT IS VALUED AT YOUR ORGANIZATION? PERFORMANCE!

Do you know what is valued on your team, in your department, in your organization? Is it meeting or exceeding sales targets? Improving customer service? Innovation? Productivity? Managing projects? Reducing costs? If you don't know, you should. Ask trusted colleagues right away! Ask a number of people in different areas, at different levels. Read annual reports, internal memos, minutes from meetings, and reports from the chief executive officer (CEO). You'll hear a consistent message. Find out exactly what your boss, team, and organization see as important and focus on how you can add value in that area. Why? Because organizations want people who add value. Because organizations want results—performance. They want people who can deliver what they say they can deliver. And you want to make sure that's your image—how others see you.

One British executive observes that corporations are actively seeking out women who can bring something *tangible* to the table. As a result, he increasingly sees women being viewed less as "*female* managers or executives" when they do bring something of value to the organization (skill at turning around a division, understanding what the competitors are doing, an outstanding sales track record in a market that's new to the company, product development and marketing). People don't pay attention to gender, just to performance.

In fact, many of the male executives we interviewed seemed to feel the same way. When asked if they saw differences in management or leadership styles between men and women, many of them reflected for a moment and said, "No, I really don't. I look for the same competencies or skills in men and women. As long as they do the job, I don't care about their gender." And they really meant it! Several of the executives we interviewed added things like, "We are so desperate for talented people who can just get the job done. We really need people with good skills. Bottom-line, results-oriented employees are always sought after."

We are always desperate for talented people. We need people with transferable skills. You don't worry about the gender or race. All you care about is whether you can get the job done: competence.

ॐ

It's getting harder to identify differences in skills. But different viewpoints come into play—different sets of experiences and different ways of doing things. Things have changed over the past five to ten years. Now I would give the same advice to everyone, regardless of gender.

⛭

I don't think of male/female. It doesn't occur to me. Competence is the key.

⛭

When I was in the military in the early to mid-1970s, there were no women in the military academies; the military was just starting to introduce women in various positions. Individuals may have particular strengths and weaknesses, but in my experience, there are no traits that are unique to a gender.

⛭

It's important not to stereotype women in the organization. I spend a lot of time on diversity; it helps companies succeed by adding a different perspective to solving complex problems. What people do as individuals is more important than trying to generalize. People bring different perspectives to thinking and solving problems, a different dimension. Something that we have to recognize is that there are real differences—and that's a good thing. Sometimes we lose sight of that. The skills that everyone brings to the table have to be outstanding, but the perspectives are different.

Think about it what value do you bring to your team, department, or organization? What are you known for? Really think about it. Can you give specific examples? You may say, "I have great communication skills." Okay, but so what? How does that add value to the team or organization? How does that help your image or visibility? Who knows what you can do? Be specific. For example, can you say that your outstanding communication skills have helped your team work more effectively and enhanced the productivity of the group? Perhaps when you took over the team or department there was constant chaos and infighting because of personality issues: People spent more time arguing and being stubborn than working on the task. But now, because of your skill, the team members work well together and projects are completed on or before schedule. You can deliver outstanding results. And now people come to you when a big project comes up because they know you can get it done with your team. That's creating value for the organization—and visibility for you.

Or you say that you have great analytical and logic skills. Okay, so? How are you using them? The next time you go to a meeting with your boss or superiors, don't just take data or statistics or research to justify what you've been doing (to introduce a new idea or support your position on a project, for example). Take it to the next step—*use* your analytical skills. Create a report that integrates the information you have gathered and offer *solutions, strategies, timelines, estimated budgets,* or *return on investment* for the organization. Spend some time thinking about outcomes and talking to others to get their input. Give your boss something to take to his or her boss. Make them look good. Create an opportunity for others to say, "Wow, I'm impressed!" Then, the next time someone asks you in an interview, "So, what are your strengths?" pull out your reports as an example.

One executive shares an example of creating an opportunity.

You have a new boss. Think about how to respond to him or her in the early weeks—be proactive; present yourself and what you are doing clearly and succinctly (and if you can't do that, do something about it). Present your objectives in a professional way (short, easy to digest). Think about how you want to come across—professional, open to new ideas and direction, an energy giver. (Remember your values. This is not about scoring points or self-publicity!) This is an example of creating an opportunity because a new boss will be keen to work with you if you respond positively, honestly, and bravely. Who knows what will happen next? Exciting, isn't it?

CHANGING IMAGE AND PERCEPTION

Image and perception are the subtle things that we need to delve into to understand; this usually is not something that's specific and tangible. What is your image? How do people see you? Some people have a sort of automatic "halo effect" based on their credentials. When you meet someone and that person is introduced as the former secretary of state or the CEO, you have a pretty good idea of who that person is and what he or she has accomplished. Others have earned the image because of the title: Doctor, General, Admiral, Ambassador.

Kathleen Hall Jamieson, dean of the Annenberg School for Communication at the University of Pennsylvania, adds an interesting insight on image in her book *Beyond the Double Bind.*[2] She cites the image of competence of two well-known yet very different women: United Nations ambassador Jeane Kirkpatrick and former senator Nancy Kassebaum.

Kirkpatrick, the intellectual, "heard her speeches dismissed as lectures, her rebuttals . . . as 'confrontations.' " In contrast to the "tough and confrontational" Kirkpatrick, Kassebaum was seen as "too traditionally female." Saying that she was someday "going to hit someone over the head for calling me diminutive and soft-spoken," she, like Kirkpatrick, was able to establish credibility.

"Kassebaum did it in the way women have traditionally used to gain political power: by invoking a family legacy—in her case as the daughter of a revered former governor and presidential aspirant. Kirkpatrick took an alternative route, gaining credentials from major universities and writing important books. Each entered the public domain with the protection of assumed competence." The lesson here? Understand that you must establish a certain set of credentials—whatever is appropriate in your environment—which can go a long way toward giving you the credibility and assumed competence you will need as you advance in your career.

In the military, when you show up at a new command with four stripes on your sleeve, everyone already knows your background, your experience. They don't necessarily know the person, but they know the position—what you obviously have accomplished and the expertise you have gained. They know that you have been through a certain experience. Trust comes from this experience—it's accepted. Of course, you can lose their trust, but it starts with the stripes. In civilian life, however, there are no outward insignias that indicate who you are and what you've done. You must earn that trust from day one.

Most people, however, especially early in their careers, have to rely on building up their accomplishments and reputations. And for many people, unless they have had early successes and many accomplishments, that takes a while. But what happens if you have already developed a certain image that's not what you want to project? Can it be changed?

Diane, a middle manager, is known for her enthusiasm but is always coming up with new ideas that generally are not taken very seriously, especially in department meetings. The impression is that the *amount* of her ideas is greater than the *quality* of her ideas; consequently, she is seen as something of a lightweight. In one meeting she came up with a really good idea, but her reputation "baggage" had become a problem. Although there was a meeting agenda, she offered her idea in the middle of the meeting. Her colleagues started rolling their eyes at each other, the "here we go again" look. Diane's boss, a bottom-line type of manager, picked up on the general mood of the meeting and put down her idea, moving on to the next agenda item.

Diane needs to work on gaining more credibility and visibility. We have all been in meetings where the attendees just want to get the information and then get back to their own issues and the crises in their departments. Managers deal with uncertainty and chaos all day long; they don't want unnecessary confusion in their world. For many, meetings are often an annoyance or a waste of time, something that takes them away from their "real work." The last thing they want to deal with is an idealist with lots of blue-sky ideas. What can Diane do?

First, she can take the first step and talk to her boss or to a trusted mentor or advocate, asking for appropriate feedback and suggestions on how she can be heard more effectively in groups or meetings. She can also observe the other team or group members: Who is heard, respected, credible? Why? Is it their style, content, preparedness? Does she need to change her communication style? How? Does she need coaching for presentations, public speaking, or seminars?

Diane needs to tighten up her range of ideas rather than constantly throwing out thoughts in meetings without considering the big picture. She can choose several ideas that she feels may have merit and then discuss them with her boss or other key team members before the meeting. She also has to find better ways to present her ideas, such as putting them on the agenda instead of offhandedly presenting them. This can prepare the group for her ideas as well as help her organize what she will present. Or perhaps she can put ideas on a Power Point presentation or overhead slide. She needs to ask for feedback as she tries out various strategies or approaches. What works? What doesn't?

Diane has to be overprepared for each meeting: She needs to do her homework and be ready for tough questions. Does she know her facts, numbers, statistics? Has she taken raw data and analyzed and synthesized them into a cohesive, understandable format or report? Does she know what competitors are doing? Can she give a budget or predict a return on investment (ROI)? She must be prepared for colleagues to be very tough on her and perhaps to challenge her ideas.

In addition, she can enlist the aid of her boss or another key group or team member who will be willing to underscore her ideas or comments, reiterating the importance of her key points or saying, "I like that idea." This doesn't happen automatically; this person should know that Diane is working to improve her group/team position or image and be forthcoming in his or her feedback. Diane also needs to be aware that these strategies will not work overnight. It took a while for her to develop her reputation as an overly enthusiastic lightweight, and so it will take at least as long to counteract that image. But she has to start somewhere. What would you do in her situation?

If you are perceived as a lightweight—not tough enough, not decisive, not a great negotiator—start by examining the situation. Identify the necessary skills. Do you already have them, or do you need to develop them? If they are skills you may need to improve, work twice as hard to improve and develop those skills and competencies. *Performance. Performance. Performance.* Take on jobs no one else wants. Volunteer to work on special projects. Go the extra mile. Do more work than you have to on your projects.

Then talk to mentors or advocates to assess your style. Is your style congruent with the organization? How will you let others know about your skills and competencies? Do you have a sponsor or advocates to spread the word? If you do not, go out and find a few. (Refer to Chapter 4 on mentoring.) Consider how you interact with team members and leaders. Do you have an effective network? Get to know key people. Seek out feedback. Observe others with a style that works in your organization and see how you can adopt it. But don't go so far to the other extreme that you will be criticized for being too over the top—customize it to your personality. Find your own style, one that works for you. It will take time, energy, effort, and advice but will pay off in the long run. Later in this chapter we'll talk more about developing your own style in the workplace.

Take a few minutes to think about these questions:

- What are your competencies and skills?
- What are you known for?
- How do others perceive you?
- Do you need to change others' perceptions of you?
- If so, how do you plan to communicate those changes?

Consider doing the following:

- Volunteer to take on projects that have measurable results.
- Talk about your successes.
- If necessary, take appropriate courses, earn a degree, or gain the required experience.
- Let others know about the experience, degrees, and accomplishments you have achieved.
- Choose mentors or advocates and let them "sing your praises."
- Write newsletters or articles and do presentations, training programs, and so forth.
- Ask for and accept feedback.
- Be aware of how others perceive you.

- Gain content expertise in appropriate areas.
- Be more prepared than you need to be.
- Be more of a risk taker.
- If appropriate, take diction or voice classes.

ARE THERE DIFFERENCES IN STYLE AND IMAGE BETWEEN MEN AND WOMEN AT WORK?

There seems to have been an evolution in the model, if you want to call it that, of women's success. Fifteen to twenty years ago the goal was getting women into positions of influence, not worrying about their style. There was only one style for success—act like a man. Then the model evolved into developing more of one's own style, as long as it fit within certain parameters—you could wear red, for example. But as recently as five or ten years ago we still looked at the barriers for women and how they could be overcome. The emphasis was on barriers, and the tone was almost one of victimhood.

I believe that we have yet again evolved to the next step: Many successful women and men say that there are far fewer barriers for women than ever before. The emphasis on performance and results and the dearth of good leadership skills have necessitated that we concentrate less on gender, race, or personality and more on skills. People don't even have to like you, but they will respect your accomplishments.

In fact, in a recent article, senior women across industries were asked, "What is power?" It was interesting to hear the definition or image of power among the various women. Here were some of the responses:

- Power is envisioning a different future and helping to make it a reality.
- Power is the freedom to work in ways I want to work.
- Money equals power.
- Power is the courage to be a woman in a man's world.
- Power goes to the partners who generate the most business.
- Power is getting on boards.
- Power is talking to employees as a leader, not as a nurturer.
- Power is reaching a certain income level or job.
- Power is the ability to influence your environment to suit your needs.

- Power is gaining the respect of men in a male-dominated environment.
- Power is having the resources available to get done what you want to do.[3]

As you can see, there are many interpretations of "power." For me, it's not about ego. I personally agree with the second definition: the freedom to work in ways I want to work, to suit my own needs. However you describe it, you're not going to get there without performance and results.

How should a woman act at work to achieve top results? This is a topic of much debate. Many people feel that performance is the only important variable and that there are essentially no differences in how successful men and women perform in corporations, the military, politics, or the professional arena. They should all be treated equally, with the major focus being on skills and results. Others, both men and women, disagree, believing that differences between men and women are the real strength of organizations and should be not only acknowledged but celebrated.

However, most people agree that *skills* are essentially the same between successful men and successful women and that there are differences in their *styles*—not necessarily better or worse, just different. A number of our participants—both men and women—agreed with this. Others actually celebrated the differences between men and women. Although we just asked the questions, "What special talents and skills do women bring to the organization?" and "What can women do to enhance their career success?" we ended up getting a lot of insights into the differences between men and women. I am aware that there are women who believe that talking about differences in style between men and women may be divisive, that it's better not to call attention to that issue, and that's all right in a perfect world. But there is a wide range of opinions out there, and I, for one, like to know what people really think. Remember, we're talking about style here, not skills. Others' impressions of your style are subjective—and your image is basically what others think it is.

Here are several thoughts that the participants had. I bet you can't tell in many cases which responses came from men and which came from women.

I've had the good fortune to work with a number of talented, strong women. I've previously had two female CFOs [chief financial officers] working for me. While they were exceptionally talented, I also felt that they were willing to work harder and apply themselves more than many others in the organization.

೧✧౨

Women bring a better balance to the perception of business. In general, their "less macho" approach enables them not to make some of the major errors. Most women don't seem to have the need to feel that they are "on top of the world," "winners," etc. They also seem to provide a more balanced team.

∾

You're at a competitive disadvantage if you don't have women on your team. The best solutions come from including a number of different perspectives. Women bring a wealth of insights and values. In terms of management skills, women in general are able to harness different types of people and focus on what's to be achieved. They seem able to engage their colleagues and capture their ideas. They "remember the plot" and have the tenacity to be "finishers."

∾

Several of the labor relations specialists in our plants were women. They had to deal with the crusty old guys, but they handled them better than men could. They don't always agree with them, but they have developed relationships, they care, they listen, they extract information.

∾

Women don't tend to give up. They seem to have a higher level of patience, endurance, and persistence.

∾

Women offer extraordinary collaborative abilities and organizational skills. They readily embrace diversity and provide a "level playing field" for job candidates. They also project a strong determination to participate in and lead successful initiatives. Women focus on the people values in all processes and consistently express a positive outlook for the future of the work group.

∾

Among the characteristics that I've observed women bringing to an organization is their attention to detail. In general terms, I felt that I could rely on the women on my staff to get projects done. Women can sometimes bring added clarity to issues as well. They can view the problem more clearly and find the best solution.

∾

Women tend to bring less ego to the table. They see things more clearly. But they need to step up to the plate, step forward to lead— sometimes they seem afraid to do that.

Women are team players. They put the success of the team ahead of their individual interests. And they care sincerely about the other members of the team both as professionals and as people.

❧

Women need to be very professional. I know that some men feel there's a double standard. I've seen this myself, mostly with senior women. Some have made sexist remarks to men (like "nice butt," etc.), or they tell off-color jokes, but the men in the room feel, "Hey, if I did that, I'd get nailed." They don't like the double standard.

From a woman's point of view, in response to the last observation above, I think that many women are in a bind—they're told that they're too soft. Or perhaps these women have been subtly told, "You're not like the guys." So they imitate men's behavior, and now they think they're one of the guys. But that doesn't work for them either; it just creates friction and resentment. (But does anyone ever tell these women they are being offensive?) They need someone to let them know that this style isn't working for them. Some women can get away with it perfectly well, but it's probably a fine line, a balance. It depends on the woman, the men, the environment, her experiences, and her colleagues' experiences. However, socialization research has shown that neither men nor women feel particularly comfortable with colleagues who are overly aggressive and domineering. Not coincidentally, we heard this advice a lot: "Don't try to be like men." These executives' (male and female) opinions mirror the research:

I would offer this advice: Don't try to imitate male colleagues. Some women do. Some are assertive, overly aggressive. They have seen men do this, and it doesn't work. In fact, I would be equally critical of men using such a dictatorial style.

❧

If I could give women any career advice, it would be to tell them not to try to be like men. Be authentic. People sense when you're not, and it makes them nervous. If you have a tendency to feel and express self-doubt, respect that feeling but use it productively to challenge yourself.

❧

Act like women—don't emulate men! You're phony if you do. Most guys I've talked to in business say the same thing. Apply what makes you unique. There's no stereotype or prototype for a leader. In my experience, none of the senior, successful women have lost their gender.

Men and women were equally candid about their observations of some men's style. Again, as we said, these are huge generalizations, and I suspect that most of the senior men we interviewed do not fit most of these stereotypes either. But as I mentioned in the introduction, it is critical to see a cross section of behaviors and styles in order to be as well prepared as possible. You can't assume that everyone comes from the same mold.

Guys often want to step on other guys. Women are more patient about getting to the answer—a good answer. And they're more passionate about their work.

∽

In negotiations, for example, women tend to look for a win/win solution, finding common ground, common interests, problem-solving. Men tend to approach negotiations from a win at all costs/take no prisoners approach, or use intimidation and pressure. Especially in a male environment, collaboration can be seen as a sign of weakness, so they often go with what they know.[4]

∽

Men need to be more sensitive to their behavior, sensitivity to language, to lack of tolerance. These can be poisonous. Fortunately, it's becoming less and less evident since there is now more mixing at all levels.

∽

Men sometimes have more of an "I'm right" attitude. But in my experience, less ego is better for running a business.

∽

Many women in my experience have been well rounded, and there's a lot less of the male, type A, aggressive approach.

∽

Women are much better at giving feedback than men, and they are stronger mentors. They provide superior development of people. They give quick and appropriate feedback; men often just let things go. In conflict resolution and negotiation women are less dogmatic, more willing to understand.

∽

Women think that we carry around a little yellow notebook with all the rules written down and that we keep it hidden from women. We don't. You just automatically know the rules of the game. No one teaches you; it's all the stuff you learn about on the playground.

ↄↄ

My teenage son and daughter are both competitive athletes. But despite her drive, she puts the emphasis on teamwork, whereas my son takes more of an attitude that winning is the only objective.

FINDING YOUR OWN STYLE

We have heard a lot about the importance of developing one's own style. Over the last twenty years it's been difficult for many women to navigate the landscape of their organizational culture. There are the rules that everyone knows, and then there are the unwritten rules. One of our clients was talking about how women are advancing in her organization. That company is known worldwide for its proactive and innovative initiatives for women. But despite about ten years of these targeted programs, women still aren't at the point that they would have expected or wanted. Why not?

I think that it's these unwritten rules that are the key. Okay, you have the skills—but do others see it? How are you perceived? What about your style? Is it congruent with the organization? What about your performance? Are you seen as competent and confident, or are you seen as a lightweight, too young, too inexperienced? Do you communicate clearly so that others can understand what you're saying? Are you considered one of the group, or are you not included in the loop? You need to get feedback on, first, what style works best in your organization, and, second, how your style measures up.

It absolutely depends on the industry, the organization, the senior management, and your boss. What works for your colleagues in another organization—or even in other departments at your organization—won't necessarily work for you.

Consider this example from baseball, long a bastion (of course, male) of competition and toughness, a place where only the strongest and best survive. Joe Torre, manager of the Yankees, epitomizes a winner but has developed his own style. He even shows emotion! Tears could be seen in his eyes as his team won the 2000 World Series. But he felt comfortable doing that, and his performance speaks for itself. He didn't lose any credibility. Yes, he has found his own style, but it wasn't always in vogue. Earlier in his managing career he thought, Should I be a hard-ass? But conflict and raw emotion don't work for him; he found that communication, honesty, and loyalty are what works.

He has brought together a collection of "rookies and retreads, recovering drug addicts and born-again Christians, Cuban defectors and defective throwers" and made them a team. "I try to understand what motivates other people," he says, and he manages more in the clubhouse than on the field, epitomizing emotional intelligence, the ability to see what moves and motivates others. He often engages in informal one-on-one talks with his players and tends to watch and listen before he says anything. Torre finds that in this way he can get a better read on what's really going on with each of his team members.[5]

Another leader found a style that works well for him.

I think a skill I have found useful is the ability to recognize talent in people, no matter how I might feel interpersonally toward a person. This means sometimes expanding my comfort zone to work with people who at times have been difficult. This does not mean compromising myself or my values or sense of self. But it does mean I examine why a particular person seems difficult for me to work with. Upon reflection, I usually find it is just my personal bias in regard to a particular personality trait. I find some people are too direct, some people are too task-focused, or whatever. But then I realize that that is just the way they are, and it is really I who have a problem with that. If I can work with that part of his or her personality, I realize the person is actually quite talented and adds a lot of value.

Sometimes I think we write people off because they don't fit our comfort zone of management or as a peer colleague. But if you limit your support and professional network only to people you are comfortable with, you severely limit your own opportunity to be successful.

∞

Look out for a tendency (which I know I have had at times) to be overly self-deprecating. Ensure through mentors (of both genders) that you don't fall into this trap. Again, it's about being as objective as you can about yourself, stripping away any tendency that you might have to reduce your self-worth in other people's eyes. Harness the warmth and empathy that women naturally have and use that to create relationships with people of both genders. It comes back to not being frightened of being yourself, being sure who you are, and finding a place for your own talents and way of working, even if it's not immediately obvious that the organization will welcome it. Believe me, if you are honest and true to yourself and enjoy some of the natural attributes of being a female, the organization will respond to you and to that style of working. It's authentic if it's you!

The qualities that have served me best in developing my leadership style have been my abilities to communicate and motivate. Absolutely critical, as well, is being genuinely enthusiastic and upbeat, no matter what. Showing the side that's tired, distracted or not engaged is not what employees want to see in a leader. I believe that people want their leaders to be out in front, showing the way.

One CEO recalled a dramatic change in his personal style, from tough as nails to a bit mellower:

As a thirty-year-old, I had a different style: I was tough as nails. I always had a lot of passion, but I had to learn how to rechannel that passion. I had to change. I'm sure that a lot of the guys above me put up with me grudgingly, but once I realized that I had to change, I did a 180-degree turn.

Some women say that their styles have changed as they have proved themselves and earned a reputation, as they have begun to feel more confident, and even their colleagues, mostly male, have changed their own attitudes.

You have the luxury of being yourself, using your own style, once you have reached a certain level, but you have to be much more aware of the style you're using while you're on the way up.

However, some women don't feel that they have had to change their personal style yet. Coincidentally, on two different occasions we met several young women in engineering—their first job out of school, working with men, many of whom were old enough to be their fathers. They added that some of these guys are very paternalistic. But these young women are very comfortable with their own style and image, and so the behavior of the men doesn't bother them. These women, who were in different companies and had never met each other, had the identical experience. They understood where the guys were coming from: "It was like working with my dad." They were very up front with how they felt; they said that "paternalistic" isn't necessarily the same as "patronizing" or "condescending." They frequently joked around with their much more mature male colleagues. They didn't get bent out of shape trying to prove a point—they didn't have to. Why? Their performance was outstanding. The guys respected their work. Their styles may have been different, but the skills were the same.

INSIGHTS FROM THE TOP

Our male executives were unanimous in their positive opinions about the women they work with: They truly respect and value their female colleagues. They admire them. They have very positive things to say about their performance and their unique skills, which they frequently underscored, saying that women contribute enormously to a positive culture. And believe me, it wasn't a matter of being politically correct—many didn't hesitate to make all kinds of observations. The message was clear: These leaders truly meant what they were saying. They value women's perspectives. They want women to be themselves, not imitate male behavior. They don't want women to change, which is contrary to what many women think they need to do.

When we share these insights with a lot of women we know, many of them say, "I wish I had had this information ten years ago—it would have made my life so much easier." I think that's true. However, to be inclusive, I am very aware that some of our readers may be initially annoyed that we are including this seemingly "paternal" advice to women. But remember that *a number of these observations were made by senior women.* Even I had to go back and look at my notes to see which quotes were from men and which were from women—the advice was nearly exactly the same.

In my career I have received advice and feedback that initially annoyed or upset me: feedback on skills, performance, communication, or style. But eventually I agreed with just about every single piece of advice that I received. It just took a while to realize how important it was. Then I worked on improving those areas. You can't take it personally. There may be things that you like and other things that you may not like. But most of the women we talk to want to know the whole picture and really want to understand what an entire cross section of their work environment looks like. I don't know about you, but I certainly want to know what people really think—I already know all the politically correct stuff. And I think that this is really useful information whether you're a man or a woman.

Don't Try to Act Like a Man

I was glad to hear this. As you read earlier, we heard this one *a lot.* I was also quite surprised that, as I mentioned earlier, a number of women, as well as men, felt that women should not act like men. Many women have complained for years that they have to act like men. However, it can be a fine line—don't be too feminine, don't be too masculine. And no, it's not fair that women have such narrow limitations in their "acceptable" behavior range, but I have seen hundreds of successful women who have mastered the skill amazingly well. Ask them for advice on developing your best personal style.

I tell my two daughters what I would tell other women: "Don't try to be like us." Don't try to emulate men; don't give orders like men. For example, when you do a Meyers-Briggs, you get a good sense of people's style, and it just reinforces what others know innately about you. If someone—either a man or a woman—tries to act like an alpha male, your employees know when you're faking it.

For example, some people, men and women, can lead with strong eyes, a quiet voice—there's a wide range of leadership styles. If women try to be alpha males, it won't work. If they're too weak, it won't work either. It takes courage for women to be heard.

Solicit (and Act upon) Feedback

We need to take good feedback less personally. Feedback is critical for success, but we have to be ready for the cold, hard facts. My opinion has always been, *If you get any feedback at all, you're doing pretty well.* Certainly, if you think it's off-base, don't get upset about it, just ask a few more people—other mentors and advocates. See if they agree. They may say, "Hey, don't listen to those jokers. They don't know what they're talking about." But if you keep hearing the same theme, maybe it's true.

Seek feedback often and openly—and act on it. Someone once said to me that "withholding feedback is a hostile act." It made me think about my attitude toward giving and getting feedback and made me work at the giving and receiving of fact-based feedback.

Get Along with Other Women

Isn't it interesting that several participants—both women and men—added that some women still seem to have difficulty working with other women? We heard this more than a couple of times: "Women can sometimes be their own worst enemies!" My opinion? I think that if we are extremely confident in our skills and competencies, there is a lot less room for jealousy or competition. The message? Performance! On a positive note, I still see large numbers of senior women who commit a great deal of time and energy to encouraging women—and men—coming up behind them through mentoring, networking, and sponsorship.

I think that women listen better, have better communication skills, and offer team-based solutions. I'm a huge advocate of diversity—I think that it makes organizations better. However, I have also observed that women can be their own worst enemies—they pick out flaws in other women. They need to work better together.

༺ঌঌ

I know that it's a generalization, but I have seen that women reporting to other women often have more difficulties than either women reporting to men or men reporting to women. I don't know what it is—jealousy? Hard to say. In my experience, men have no problem working for a woman they respect and trust.

༺ঌঌ

As children, boys learn to be friends with their opponents. Their games are more competitive, violent and conflictual than girls'. If little boys did not become friends with their opponents, they would soon have no friends, because their opponents one day are their teammates the next. Out of necessity, the boys learn to separate their play from their friendships. Because little girls avoid conflict in their games, they have no compelling reason to learn this separation.[6]

Be Aware of Your Communication Style

Something that hit home with me was hearing, "Some women may want to work on keeping their thoughts more succinct." I'm really outgoing and high-energy, and so I know that this is something I have to rein in every once in a while. I used to think, Well, everyone knows my personality. They don't care. But they do. You have to adapt to the environment. It can take a long time to change this behavior, but I suggest carefully watching and listening to people who have outstanding communication styles, taking lots of notes—and practicing!

Let me give you an example of communication styles. In a male audience, men are much tougher and more critical of women than they are of other men—their gestures, tone, speaking style, dress, behavior, etc. The substance of what they're saying often gets lost. It's unfortunate, but it's important to be aware of some people's perceptions and work on developing outstanding communication skills— and get feedback on how you're doing.

༺ঌঌ

On our team there is a woman about whom I often heard comments on how quickly she spoke. The perception was, "We can't understand her, but I guess it doesn't really matter what's she's saying anyway." I brought it to her attention and worked with her to address the issue, and the results were tremendous.

⌘

I might offer an observation: If you ask for an answer, sometimes you can get a War and Peace *answer. Some women may want to practice being a bit more succinct.*

Develop Your Own Personal Style

Many of our participants underscored the importance of developing a style that works for you. They suggested observing others with a style that works in their organization and customizing it to one's personality.

I think that most women are more mature, thoughtful, and willing to understand. Although I believe that women are different from men, I don't think that there are any differences in skills. I don't think that women should hide—or accentuate—the differences. It should be based on what they deliver, just like men. Is it easier for men? Maybe sometimes—men have a lot of others to relate to. But I would say, "Be yourself, be professional. And don't allow others to treat you unprofessionally." Women should be proud of being women but also use the skill sets they have to achieve recognition.

⌘

Use your own special strengths. If you can't engage people, you won't get the best from them. At the end of the day they must trust you, believe in you, and respect you in order to cause change. And this is built over years, not days. It takes time. You have to cause people to want to follow you.

⌘

It's important for women to be assertive in a positive way. With a deliberate, calm manner you can convey that you can do the job even if you don't feel 100 percent confident.

⌘

My advice to women? Develop a style that men are comfortable with.

⌘

If there is any impediment to women's success that I've observed, it's more in the sense of perception by others (usually men) that they are "too something." In their evaluations, they are perceived as too soft, too aggressive, not at the right level of whatever. This seems to occur in Europe, the United States, and Latin America, although less so in Asia. They must fight to overcome that male stereotype.

∽

I think it's important for women to develop a style that men are comfortable with. Become an expert at negotiating the political landscape.

Develop Key Skills

This comes back to performance. As I mentioned earlier, this was one of the main themes I heard in the research. Be attentive to discovering which skills and competencies are most valued in your organization, and if you aren't yet skilled in those areas, start working at it. Again, keep in mind that some of these comments were made by senior women.

In my industry, I've observed that in general, men excel at talking and selling but are not quite as strong as women in terms of execution. Women seem to make a strong contribution with their execution, follow-through, planning, and organizing. If I had to make a recommendation, women would be well served to focus on their presentation, negotiation, and influencing skills—"the talking." This is the way to gain visibility, which is key. Being good at what you do is a prerequisite, but influencing others and gaining visibility and recognition are key to climbing the ladder.

∽

Take on difficult and hard-to-do things. People tend to underestimate this, even in the United States. It gives you more visibility. People don't do this as much in the United Kingdom. There's often less competitiveness. There's a tendency to take on jobs that are more predictable, safe, and comfortable. But if you look at underdogs who have made it to the top, you often see a common element: What did they do to succeed that the MBAs didn't? They took jobs others didn't want to take.

SUMMARY

Success Secret #2: Create an Image and a Style That Work for You

◆ Make sure that your image is "I work hard. I deliver results. I'm interested in bottom-line performance." You can have great flexibility in your style and personality as long as you get results.

◆ Identify what is valued in your organization, in your department, and on your team. If you don't know, find out right away.

◆ Get feedback from trusted others about your image in the workplace. It may surprise you. How do others see you? Is your image congruent with the organization's goals or mission? If it is not, start working on it right away.

◆ Develop a style that allows you to be heard. Among our participants there were few differences seen between men and women regarding skill—more differences in style. Do you adapt your communication style to the situation? Do you know your boss's or colleagues' values, hot buttons, issues, interests? Make it a point to learn them.

◆ Bring something tangible to the table. Women are viewed less as "*female* managers or executives" when they can bring something of value to the organization (skill at turning around a division, understanding what the competitors are doing, an outstanding sales record in a market that's new to the company, product development and marketing, etc.). People don't pay attention to their gender, just to their performance.

For a list of research participants, please see page xvii.

Define Your Role as a
Team Leader or Participant

◦◐◦

I led a team of incoming plebes [at West Point] during basic training. I thought I had to lead the way that I saw others doing it—with stress and shouting, like a traditional drill sergeant. Well, my unit performed very badly. And they hated me. That experience shook me up. I realized that leadership isn't rule-based. It isn't about stress. It's about inspiration, about setting and communicating a vision. It's about gaining trust. Once you have someone's trust, once you get them on the same sheet of music, they don't want to disappoint you. Then leading becomes very easy.[1]

—Christina "C.J." Juhasz, U.S. Military Academy

People frequently are faced with situations which necessitate a team approach rather than simply making a quick individual decision: task forces, new initiatives, crises, new product design and development, and so on. How do we begin? Whom do we choose? Who is going to perform? What is our team-building process? What is our timeline or deadline? Whether you're a team leader or a team member with your eyes on a leadership position in the future, the insights in this chapter will be useful.

BUILDING AND DEVELOPING THE TEAM: THE PROCESS

Most seasoned team leaders say that you first need to examine the goals and the reasons for developing the team. Then you can begin to choose the players: Who will create the best fit? Who has the talent, the experience, the potential to succeed? Who will work well together? Should you use existing people or bring in new team members?

When building a team, whether you take on a new position, a new assignment, or a new initiative, the process begins with understanding the mission and goals, understanding the people, and balance. First, you need to understand the area of responsibility you have taken on. What is going on in the environment, internal and external? Then start to see if the current players are up to it: Do they understand what has to be done? Do they have what it takes to get it done, and do they understand the challenges? Are they capable of working as a team? Do they have the ability to get results? The motivation? You must also ask yourself if it is more advantageous to develop the current players or introduce new blood. You really have to examine the characteristics, skills, dynamics, and experience of potential team members.

Once you have established (or assessed) the team makeup, you want to set the tone: What should the team members expect from you, and what can you expect from them? This process can serve to assess the tenor of the group, gauge skills and talent. You want to start to get to know each other, to build relationships. There are numerous venues, from doing a team-building assessment such as the Meyers-Briggs, to structured "get to know each other" meetings, to getting together for casual lunches.

One senior executive says she likes to use the Meyers-Briggs to get a sense of the team. It identifies different personality and communication types, and that is helpful when she wants to get a sense of who the more creative members are, or the more tactical members, or who can keep everyone motivated and upbeat, especially during a crisis or with a deadline looming.

Another executive makes it a point to try to meet with the team members individually before they start the project to get a sense of their strengths, weaknesses, and interests. This way, he can help head off personality or performance problems that otherwise might blindside him down the road. He adds:

You've got to remember that a team is made up of individual members, all of whom want to feel valued and able to contribute. But also, certain personalities sometimes just don't work together. I've had people who are control freaks and can't deal with constantly ongoing issues—they need closure. Or others who think that they're doing more than everyone else—if I don't address it to their specific satisfaction, they get upset. I confess that sometimes I've just been too busy to constantly hand-hold them. But looking back, had I addressed it at the time, it probably would have been easier in the long run.

However you choose to do it, it is important to get a sense of these personalities, issues, values, baggage, hot buttons, the ways they like to work, previous experiences, expectations, and motivation. Set the tone, develop the culture of the team, and share your vision as the team leader. Develop a good mix of individuals.

A senior executive at a European high-tech company shared his experience with identifying specific team leadership at his company.

I found that it was necessary to "fast-track" our presence in the United States, and so I decided that it was better to bring in an outsider from my previous network, someone I knew well, who already had a proven track record in achieving what needed to be done in that market. He was a known commodity, and so I felt that it minimized the downside risk of choosing the wrong person.

In the product management and software development area, however, I decided that it was better to keep the current players and help them raise their game. With the critical need to get product to market quicker and better, I felt more comfortable keeping and developing people who knew the company products and culture/style. Bringing in outsiders in these areas undoubtedly would have taken some time to get them up to speed on products and process, which could have risked momentum being lost in the development process—critical in a high-tech arena.

Another senior executive described her first month as the leader in her new job and the qualities she looked for in her new team members.

My first order of business was to set the priorities for myself and my management team. My first priority was to "stabilize the patient." I wanted to deliver an overall operational plan, which did not currently exist. In addition, I developed one version of a monthly business report. When I arrived, there were multiple versions of financial reports and no way to accurately measure our current status against our goals. The team up to that point was unable to determine where we were against the forecast. (Were we 5 percent above? Ten percent below? There was no way to accurately assess our actual performance versus our forecast.) I looked for people who had the right skills and a commitment to deliver results.

One senior member of a pre-IPO (initial public offering) company described how teams generally are put together, outlining techniques that can be adapted to any new team. As opposed to an established company in which there is usually a clearly identified job to be done, in an IPO a team is put together from scratch, and it needs to be a "smart" team that brings a variety of expertise and talent to complement each member's abilities. He believes that investors generally are looking for a collective resource and leadership pool to make a company successful rather than a specific group of bosses as such. There is less of an emphasis on "one god" at the top.

Here, for example, the top team consists of a CEO, who is primarily there as an expert to attract the funding and as someone with the personality to bring in strong people to create a top team without feeling personally threatened. Also, there is the original founder, who has confessed he has little management ability—he thinks that he can act as an evangelist both inside and outside the company but would make a "crap manager." Then there is a guy who has been in the business for fifteen years and managed strategy for one of the leading operators in the field. Plus a "geek" from another company who knows all about backbone, infrastructure, etc., and can devise IT [information technology] strategy for the business. And then there is me, whom the other members see as someone who knows how to run a business, plus has a proven track record in getting things done and has experience in analyzing and revising the strategic direction of a business, if necessary.

IDENTIFYING TEAM LEADERSHIP ABILITIES

A number of the leaders we interviewed said that it's a challenge to identify the potential leaders in an organization and then to motivate those potential leaders and allow the employees who probably will never be leaders to grow and develop to their fullest potential. It's usually pretty easy to identify the 5 to 10 percent at the top, but identifying the potential skills of the other 90 percent is tricky. Bosses, mentors, advocates, and sponsors need to pay careful attention to the employees to identify latent skills and competencies as well as encourage them to develop additional expertise. Several of our participants, for example, encouraged their staff members to go back to school to earn a degree. Others have tried to give them stretch assignments or have recommended them for highly visible teams. But team members need to be prepared for the leadership call as well.

Truly believe in the value of teamwork. Teamwork is a cliché, but in a cliché often lies truth. You cannot know everything, cannot be everywhere, cannot be all things to all people. You not only need to know how to build high-performance teams, you also need to know how to function as a team member. No one wants you on the team if you don't have a skill that complements the group.

Team leaders often look to the strongest, most qualified member for a particular assignment—the most qualified in skill, experience, or, in some cases, literally in strength. During the September 11 attack five firefighters in one ladder company were together and got the order to evacuate. On a high floor they encountered an older woman who was having difficulty moving down the stairs. The captain of the company realized that because of her frailty, one of his men was going to have to support most of the woman's weight down the sixty-eight floors. Although every man on the team was strong and fit, the captain chose the person he felt could do the best job. He said, "Billy was my biggest guy, so I assigned him to the task."

Many of our participants talked about their experiences in identifying team leadership skills. Here are several of their comments:

I've always been involved in baseball, well, for about forty to fifty years. First in Little League, now in coaching, and the scenario never changes. On every team there are always one or two kids who are really great. Then there are probably five or so who are pretty good. There are another two or three who are okay, then another two or three who are not very good. And I see the same percentages all the time in business. The best team members will always do well, but every CEO has the issue of motivating—and getting the best from— the other members of the team.

◌◌◌

We hired 250 new managers last year. You can tell by the end of the first year who is going to succeed. But usually you can tell a lot faster than that. Starting from scratch, I identify which members will work together well based on their skills and their alignment or fit with the organization, team, division, or department rather than simply relying on their job titles. I look for someone I can count on. I look for someone who is aligned with the common goal of the team—they know the goal, they're in sync with the goal. My job as team leader is to always keep everyone focused on what the goal is. It's constant reinforcement, reminding them, keeping them on target. I also have to be aware that you can't always handpick your ideal team. There are often political reasons; as in a merger or acquisition, you have to be well represented by both companies. You may not know a lot of the players from the other company, so you don't know how they think or act. Some members are higher maintenance. Others will simply never deliver—they're just not capable. I usually look for someone who can "pinch-hit," who's willing to take ownership of some of the issues.

ॐ

Being an officer in the military taught me the value of teamwork and diversity. Everybody thinks of the Marines as being authoritarian, but it's not. It's team-oriented. I had thirty-one men in my first command, most of whom were disadvantaged minorities without a high school diploma. But you learned that disadvantaged didn't mean that they weren't smart. They had innate intelligence and character. You saw who the natural leaders were. You just had to recognize their skill sets and bring out those individual strengths of your team members.

For some team participants, being tagged early on by a senior member of the organization as a "high-potential worker" can bring enormous benefits.

My mentor has gotten me involved in highly visible teams—he's a huge advocate of diversity and saw my potential. I admit that not only have I gained terrific experience with these opportunities and increased my visibility, I've also acquired a greater sense of self-confidence from the exposure.

ॐ

As you hire people, get the best you can find—the smartest, the most capable. Some people can be uncomfortable with or intimidated by this approach, but in reality, the best people will only make you look better.

In our interviews, a number of participants shared their ideas on what they look for in team members. Here are some of the characteristics:

◆ Performance-focused
◆ Able to deliver (able to actually do the job)

- Willing to do the job
- Experienced
- Good fit for the position
- Action-oriented
- Committed
- Strong work ethic
- Intellectual horsepower
- Results-driven
- Self-confident
- Good decision maker
- Good attitude
- Adaptable
- Good listener

MOTIVATING YOUR TEAM, ESPECIALLY IN A CHALLENGING ENVIRONMENT

Most people have been on teams that have a tight deadline; in that situation you don't have the luxury of strategizing, assessing, and experimenting with what will work. And in many organizations you move from team to team with lightning speed, being assigned to the next project team before you have completed the project you're working on. Especially for new team managers, this can be daunting. What do you do?

First, you probably want to touch base with a mentor or a few advocates who may be able to give you a few key tips. Let them give you advice on what has worked for them: what to do and what not to do. They may be able to provide you with good resources. It can also be good to be able to let off steam or commiserate at times.

Next, you want to be sure that there's an environment of open communication. Tension can really be high when there's a deadline and a lot of pressure, and so you should develop a system that works for the team: Will there be structured time every day to share progress reports and assessments, or do you need to meet more often in a more ad-hoc situation? Choose a communication venue: Do you need to meet in person, or can you communicate via e-mail or even by voice mail for updates? What about when there's an immediate problem for team members? Is there a hotline or contact person, a buddy, a subteam they can contact immediately so that their process isn't impeded? What about distractions? When you're working long hours, it's important to schedule breaks: a pizza, a quick video game competition, a game of pool, or a few minutes in the lounge listening to music.

You also want to allow for some fun. Sometimes it helps to get together outside of work; it develops camaraderie and relationships. This can be critical when everyone is tired, cranky, and at the end of their rope. When you have gotten to know people better, it's easier to write off temporary bad tempers.

Sometimes radical new ideas can be used or modified to address the fast-paced, crazy environments found in many project teams. A few years ago Walter Noot, head of production for Viewpoint DataLabs International (which makes three-dimensional models for film, video game, and car manufacturers), realized that his young, highly talented (and highly sought after) project managers were being lured away by competitors. To keep them happy in an era of fierce competition, he resorted to a radical decision—changing the way projects worked. First, the team members do not make a salary; they're paid as if they were contract workers. Every project's team splits 26 percent of the money the company expects to receive from the client. Salaries, of course, skyrocketed, but so too did productivity. The groups used to have set hours; now the members work when they please. One guy works twenty-four-hour to thirty-six-hour marathons, keeping a pillow and blanket under his desk for when he wants to take a quick nap. Some people work only at night. Noot says that now he never hears complaints, attitudes have changed, and productivity is amazing.[2] Will it work for your project teams? Maybe, maybe not. But it's interesting to see if any of the elements can be modified for your purposes.

Some of our participants shared their team experiences:

I have a philosophy about what motivates major performances and how that should be rewarded. Although everybody likes money, people aren't necessarily motivated by cash, trips, toys, and trinkets. They want the recognition that at least once in their life they made a difference and contributed to a world-class effort—their equivalent of a gold medal.

∽

You can use the example of an "Apollo 13" type of achievement to describe teamwork in bringing about success in the face of challenge and/or adversity. One time I even arranged an off-site event at NASA's mission control in Houston for a large meeting of global managers to illustrate that message, comparing headquarters to mission control and regional directors to the astronauts.

In the pharmaceutical industry, for example, you may be able to give employees the opportunity to rise through the organization, with the associated title and money, by being a technical expert. A scientist, for example, might be more motivated by having the opportunity to innovate and to work with other world-class scientists than by being a manager or leader of other employees.

∾

Many of my team's projects are stressful and have tight deadlines. One of my biggest jobs is trying to keep employees happy—making them feel valued, feel that they are contributing. Most of the time I try to do this one on one with them, talking to them individually. I think they really appreciate that.

∾

I value talking straight, particularly in tough times. People want to know where you're coming from, what goals you've set, and what is expected of them. You earn their trust by communicating clearly and keeping your word.

Mark Loehr, chief executive officer (CEO) of SoundView Technology Group, a high-tech investment bank, chose a different strategy after the September 11 tragedy. He announced that on September 20, all the profits from that day would go to victim relief. As he personally manned the trading desk with his staff that day, the profits totaled more than $6 million (the previous one-day high had been $1.2 million). But more important was the effect of this gesture on company morale.[3]

Another executive shared this story about leading his team in challenging times.

A few years ago I was in charge of the construction of a major multimillion-dollar research center for my company in the United Kingdom. Because of heated arguments among the contractors, the architects, and the company, the consensus of the team was, "It's going to be impossible to get this job done." But the opening ceremony had already been arranged, to be attended by Queen Elizabeth, a number of Nobel laureates, and other dignitaries. Faced with a seemingly impossible goal, workdays of fifteen to eighteen hours, participants at each other's throats, personality issues, and a looming deadline, I was looking at a challenge.

However, I find that you can tell a lot about a person's leadership potential by putting that person in a non-business-related environment. I'm a strong proponent of using friendly athletic activities and team-building exercises. Because of this impasse, I decided to design an Outward Bound–type "rope course weekend" that would include the key players from the three respective parties: contractors, architect, and the corporate team. After fifteen to eighteen hours a day of screaming at one another in a work setting, I wanted to get them into another environment to build a cohesive team. The motto of the weekend was "Failure Is Not an Option."

Upon returning from that weekend, the entire team had changed. By the end of the next week construction plans were in place for the project. We were no longer three different entities; rather, it was a team effort. Through introspection, the team members learned trust, and you could see the results-oriented commitment in their eyes. Although we had to fine-tune the organizational chart a bit through intervention, caring, and giving resources and responsibilities, the job got done one week ahead of schedule.

The Importance of Maintaining Your Team in Times of Crisis

You've always wondered how you'd handle it. A crisis hits. You're the person in charge. Do you rise to the occasion? Or do you freeze up, wallow in self-doubt, or otherwise fumble your chance to shine?

Being a boss is not the same as being a leader. As I'm writing this, the entire country is still reeling from the September 11 attack on the World Trade Center. Still, in the middle of this unbelievable crisis, there have been examples of Americans' overriding need to overcome adversity and show leadership. In times of crisis, leaders need to be visible.

Ed Vick, former CEO of Young & Rubicam Advertising and a decorated Vietnam veteran, illustrated this leadership quality after the World Trade Center attack. "He greeted employees in the lobby of the company's midtown Manhattan headquarters. Nothing elaborate—simply a welcome back and how are you. Yet the gesture elicited a flood of gratitude over the following days that 'just blew me away,' says Vick."[4]

Another leader shared his perspective:

You need to look like you're confident and let your actions reflect your words. Let people know that they are cared about. A company often shows its true colors in a crisis. Also, people can take the bad news—it's better to tell your team "the way it is." They can take it if they know you're looking out for them.

In addition, an interesting aspect of this crisis to me was the part that technology played in keeping the team members in contact, allowing the leaders to lead from a distance. Many executives were stranded away from their headquarters and relied on technology to keep in touch with their teams. Bob Nardelli, chief executive officer of Home Depot, and several of his executives monitored the company's disaster relief efforts with wireless gadgets. Nardelli sent e-mails through his pager and left a company-wide e-mail for employees.

Other executives used cell phones, pagers, e-mail, and other technology essentials to manage the crisis. However, the key to these leaders' crisis management was communication.

Rand Blazer, the CEO of KPMG Consulting, shared a fascinating story with me that demonstrates the critical role leaders can play in a time of crisis. On September 11, 2001, there were over 250 of his people in the World Trade Center and also in the surrounding buildings. There were fifteen people at the Pentagon. Blazer praised his team.

What was great about our team was that there were leaders in New York and D.C. who quickly assessed that something was wrong and immediately organized a central center for action and information. Within minutes they took action and told everyone to evacuate. Not only at the World Trade Center and the Pentagon but at the State Department, White House, etc. Managing partners Sarah Diamond, Dan Johnson, and Rich Roberts took the leadership roles and organized the operation, establishing a sort of command center.

As soon as the event occurred, there were individual leaders throughout the organization who assessed, acted, and reacted quickly, saying, "I think we have a situation here. Let's move, let's get out, start making your way home. . . ." Many of the employees were on the sixty-something floor. Our employees were told to ignore the statements that it was okay to return to work—they were told, "Just get down to the ground floor." Our many leaders that day looked at the situation quickly and systematically, using a model: diagnosis, interpretation, decision making, execution. Every employee in the World Trade Center was safely evacuated. In addition, a call was made to every major KPMG Consulting office in the United States, often getting people out of bed and telling them what to do. In San

Francisco, for example, we told our people, "Stay at home today—work from home, stay out of the downtown."

These leaders were able to diagnose the situation on the spot and move and react. They realized that action can save people's lives—and certainly in this case, it did. Our corporate culture is that we have to have leaders across the environment; leadership is decentralized—it's not by accident that they took the leadership roles in a crisis and did it well. And it was not necessarily senior management. Segment or industry leaders took charge of situations, made quick decisions, and acted. Employees at the consultant level wouldn't leave until everyone was accounted for.

I asked Blazer if he felt that his personal—and positive—experience as a military officer has helped him become a role model, making an impact on the corporate culture and filtering down and encouraging this type of leadership. He said, "I don't want to take credit for these leaders' actions. It wasn't a corporate decision. These individuals did an amazing job they assessed the situation and acted immediately." A true leader, giving credit to his team and not taking credit himself. I believe that his experience has greatly influenced the culture overall; one of the underlying themes at KPMG Consulting is to encourage leadership at all levels. "It is not bureaucratic; they don't have to go up and down the ladder; there is a clear delegation of leadership."

GIVING GOOD DIRECTION TO YOUR TEAM

In an article in *Across the Board* magazine, author Gary Klein asks, "Why Won't They Follow Simple Directions?"[5] As he points out, this may be what many leaders are asking themselves, but sometimes the directions are the problem! I concur. For example, one senior executive I know has a habit of being vague:

"I'm going to a meeting with the president in an hour. I need a report on the latest sales figures." But what sales figures did she want? This quarter? Year to date? This year versus last year? By territory? For key accounts only? Domestic versus international? Hmmm, sound familiar?

Specifically, why don't many leaders simply and clearly convey what they want done by their subordinates? Klein identified several issues in giving one's team directions, the first of which is that leaders often give orders for specific actions rather than providing a framework or an explanation for why they want those actions done. There are many things that are clear only in context. Klein shared a situation in which military team leaders at the Army War College and the National Defense University were given a task to complete which would be timed and competitive.

Most of the team leaders, anxious to get a head start on the competition, rushed through their instructions and got everyone working. As one might imagine, there were a lot of questions and subteams going off in the wrong direction, misunderstanding what the team leader wanted, causing time delays and frustration. However, one leader spent fifteen minutes making sure that everyone knew exactly what the task was and what he wanted. Despite the time constraints, he didn't rush. His team didn't go off in the wrong direction and didn't make costly errors. They were effective because they received clear direction from the beginning.

Interestingly, one of the other teams started the first day's activities with only ninety seconds of direction. Of course, there were lots of mistakes that day. The next day the team leader took ten minutes for direction, and on the third he spent fifteen minutes. He learned from his mistakes, realizing that spending the time planning and giving direction pays off down the road. The lesson? Don't be rushed.

One of our participants shares the following insight:

It's not a good idea to let everyone believe that you know everything, that you have all the answers. They may look to you for guidance or direction, but the truth is that your team members probably know a lot more about specific issues than you do. Everyone has a different role; they are all experts in their own areas. My job is to bring everything together and put it into perspective and keep them focused—with a strategic goal in mind.

Klein listed the following suggestions for providing clear directions to teams or individuals. The same strategies apply whether you are giving instructions to a colleague, a direct report, or a team of twenty.

♦ First, don't give lots of unnecessary details. Too many details can further confuse what you want to accomplish, and you also want to encourage independent thinking within the given guidelines. Let the other person(s) come up with interesting ways of getting the job done. You just want the results.

♦ Second, while you want to provide some reasoning as to why you want the team to do something, keep it concise. Don't give them a laundry list of reasons.

♦ Third, don't feel that you have to give the team your vision of what the outcome will be. If you have a clear idea, fine, but if not, anticipated outcomes may be enough.

♦ Fourth, don't confuse encouragement or cheerleading with intent. Rather than simply saying something like, "Our goal is to be number one," provide a strategy or specific goals.

One executive added his thoughts on effective team leadership:

In building the team, you have to reinforce the idea that they are running the show, but keep your hands on the strings so that events proceed in the way you want until you can release control gradually. This should come as the individuals' and the team's confidence grows. Keeping the individuals focused on their key priorities in the early days is critical; this helps reinforce what their collective effort is and how each of their departmental functions contributes to it.

It is also a good idea to encourage the team to meet and decide on things and push initiatives forward without being involved yourself. When you do have formal meetings (I do it monthly here), make sure that they are well planned and highly productive.

CHANGING TEAM DYNAMICS

Over the past decade or two, of course, significant strides have been made to encourage a more diverse mix of gender, culture, race, and age in management teams across industries. It's no surprise that more diverse teams reflect the increasingly diverse markets of many organizations. But more to the point, decisions based on a wide range of perspectives are generally more targeted and effective. Here are some examples:

If you want a quick and easy decision or outcome, choose a homogeneous team. If you want depth or diversity of perspectives, choose a heterogeneous team, but expect a more drawn-out discussion and process.

∾

A mid-level executive at a large American automotive company was convinced that his company could build its international facilities more efficiently by using local talent and resources. Deciding to test this perspective when given the responsibility of building a new plant in Mexico, he used local architects to design a building reflecting local tastes. In addition to earning the respect of the locals (and consequently increasing the positive image of the company as a whole), the company was able to hire and retain local workers. The bottom line? A different perspective resulted in increased success for the organization.[6]

∾

When I took on my new position, I needed to build a cohesive team. In eighteen months I had to fire several people who were dysfunctional leaders. In order to get a team to work together well, sometimes you have to make changes. (Even Jack Welch fired some of his best friends.) I agree with Sam Walton, who says that to succeed as a manager, anyone with an IQ of 120 to 125 can probably solve any problem that arises. But to develop greatness, you have to identify how they operate as a team.

One of our participants shares the significance of changing team dynamics. Realizing the changes in its internal and external environment, the Bank of Montreal developed a ten-year transition plan designed to create more effective gender balance in its top management. Originally the bank was very male-dominated, but the CEO undertook a formal initiative which underscored the importance of gender balance. To bring the numbers in line, they asked questions such as, "What are the barriers? Is there a problem in the pipeline? The pool? Is there bias in the selection process?"

After careful planning and implementation, the bank evolved from a group of all men ten years earlier to a mix. Among the top fifty positions, twenty-four were women and twenty-six were men. It became evident that a mixed group was more effective in problem solving. There was greater consideration of issues. Things were thought of in different ways. "It felt different." As a result, the Bank of Montreal was one of the first Catalyst Award winners and was the only Canadian company at that time to win.

On the other side of the world, Ernst and Young Australia's CEO, Brian Schwartz, won the EOWA (Equal Opportunity for Women in the Workplace) Award for further improving the gender balance at senior levels in that firm. Competing with more than 2,500 companies, Ernst and Young has doubled the number of female partners thus far in his three-year term as CEO.

However, these changes in team dynamics can occur at all levels of an organization.

A while ago we all went through a team-building exercise. I don't think there was any question about my style—I'm an ex-Marine with Vietnam experience. We talked about personality types. There were four personality types that the trainers identified, like controlling, analytical, etc. The trainers described them to us, and then other people put Post-its on your back, with comments on what type they thought you were, so you couldn't see their assessment. It was really eye-opening. I realized I can't deal with every person the same way. It's stuff you know but don't really think about. I'm tough with people, and I used to see others as weak if they weren't as tough in dealing with people as I was. Now I feel differently. I realize that there are other ways of doing things, and the same results can be achieved. I thought that the process was excellent.

∾

If you have a situation with one woman and five men, for example, the dynamics can create more positive competition. I enjoy working in that kind of environment.

PROJECT MANAGEMENT

Most experts will tell you that managing projects well is the key to success. One example which epitomizes the evolution of the "project" occurred in November 2001, when Bill Gates introduced Microsoft's new game console, Xbox, amid incredible hype. Robbie Bach, senior vice president of the games division, gained another title: "Chief Xbox Officer at Microsoft." That pretty much summed up the dimension and scope of his role: enormous.

Tom Peters agrees. "One key to growing your power is to recognize the simple fact that we now live in a project world. Almost all work today is organized into bit-sized packets called projects. A project-based world is ideal for growing your brand: projects exist around deliverables, they create measurables, and they leave you with braggables. If you're not spending at least 70% of your time working on projects, creating projects, or organizing your (apparently mundane) tasks into projects, you are sadly living in the past. Today you have to think, breathe, act and work in projects."[7]

Many of the leaders we talked to shared stories of how high-potential employees took on a project, were successful, gained visibility, and then were promoted or given further responsibility. They feel that an employee has a decided advantage in the workplace if he or she has had leadership experience early on—most specifically, leading teams, making decisions, and bringing people together. Their opinion? The earlier in your career, the better.

In our organization we have a formal leadership development program that includes several components. We provide three-month rotations, the opportunity to be a project leader of cross-functional teams, line responsibilities. This provides an opportunity to learn new skills and demonstrate leadership ability. More informally, I pick a couple of more recent hires to participate on teams to get different perspectives. It also gives them a chance to learn by making smaller mistakes.

However, the key is not only managing the process but managing the people.

Sometimes it's difficult to see how your contributions affect the organization; you don't get much feedback. That's why project work is very important early in your career. I worked on a joint project with a customer earlier in my career. It was fascinating to gain insight into how both parties had different views of the same issue, both of which were very sound. It gave me a chance to see how the paradigms of each organization impacted their perspectives.

ᴼᷣᷤ

To have a successful organization you need to find the best people overall, not just in the management ranks. Motivate people by assigning them to interesting and important projects, projects aimed at reducing expenses or developing new processes.

An interesting example of project management comes from DuPont's Leadership for Growth program, which creates teams from the company's top executives to do project work on any of DuPont's product groups. As in many corporations, DuPont is made up of over 200 of these product groups within twenty-one business units, some of them as large as Fortune 500 companies. One manager states, "Working for one of these units is like living in a college dorm: You know the kids on your floor, but you don't know the ones at the other end of the building. Leadership for Growth is a way of tapping the enormous knowledge base that lurks within DuPont." These teams allow the members of the group to attack the issue at hand, utilizing collective brainpower. One program manager adds, "The recommendations that come out of these groups are as good as, if not better than, anything we get from external consultants."

How does it work? Team members are selected from among the 400 top managers to work on a specific project, one that is not in their area of expertise. The first rule of the program is this: Throw everybody into the deep end. No team member is assigned to a project within his or her division, and each person brings different skills and a different background to the effort.

These three-week-long projects focus on a wide range of ideas, from "What are new uses for Kevlar?" to "the viability of plastic beer bottles." This interesting concept is used not only as an effective training tool but also as an intelligence-gathering, idea-generating opportunity which can develop strategies that allow the viability of new products and services worth millions of dollars to be examined. The teams are assigned a coach/facilitator to help work through the process, allowing the facilitator to indirectly take refresher courses on decision making and conflict resolution. The participants, who generally know little about the product, are given three-inch binders containing product data and the results of market research as well as funding to go anywhere in the world to gather additional intelligence.

At the end of the project, suggestions to senior management are made by the team on the viability of the product, potential applications, production, markets, demographic data, possible partnerships, outlets, joint ventures, and the like, providing incredibly valuable information.[8]

Lauren Martin of Hewlett-Packard provides a clear, comprehensive, and systematic model for managing projects. She has been on more than twenty-five project teams in the last ten years and has created a checklist of questions to ask yourself before choosing a project. Here are five of the most important questions on her list:

♦ **Do you know what "done" means?** Projects need clear goals that get written down in advance, and part of doing a good job is delivering what you promised. If your objectives aren't clear, people can take really good work and sully it.

♦ **Do the heavy hitters care?** Every project wants top-management support, but few get it. Work only on those which do. Top managers will build interest in and commitment to your work.

♦ **Do the bean counters care?** Ask yourself, If the project doesn't have sufficient resources, what business value does it deliver? If it isn't important enough to fund, do you really want to spend your time on it?

♦ **Can you make fast decisions?** Schedules almost always drive projects. Fewer people, greater clarity—that's the formula for success.

♦ **Can your team members make (full) time?** In my experience, a person can contribute to no more than three projects at the same time.[9]

One executive shares his experience:

It is critical to make the most of an opportunity to lead a significant project. The example that comes to mind is that of a woman in our organization who was given the chance to develop a particular market. She was given some investment dollars to put together the research and marketing and to build a team to service the offering.

The catch was that the market didn't exist and she would have to be careful not to infringe on a similar service offering we already provided. She did a lot of networking and working the potential client base to determine how best to position the new offering. She did a lot of internal work to gain support for her approach and ideas on how the offering would be positioned. She also did some research on the current service offerings to make sure she was not stepping on any toes. Finally, she started to assemble the team that would support her in the market.

She did all this within budget and on time. It was a great success, and it moved her to the next level of leadership.

What If You're Not the Boss? Influencing Your Team

More and more frequently teams are cross-functional, which means that you, as a team leader, have far less actual control over the team. You can't hire, fire, or discipline them—you can only use your influence. It may be an international team, a cross-functional team, a team of outside vendors, or a group of individual projects coming together under you. Or you may have some authority, but the people you lead, like "software engineers, hotshot Gen Xers marketers, whoever—respond to directives the way a cat responds to the command 'roll over.' " What do you do? Several researchers have discussed this increasingly important issue—situations in which you do not have command authority.

Roger Fisher and Alan Sharp call their model lateral leadership, or leading from the side.[10] Jay Conger at the Leadership Institute at the University of Southern California dubs it management by persuasion. Whatever you may call it, the *Harvard Business Review* identifies several strategies that can be learned and practiced by anyone, whether a boss or not.

First, of course, leadership is more than a title or formal authority. As many of the leaders we interviewed agreed, it's a matter of trust and respect, which are earned over time. For leaders to have good "followship," they need to listen thoughtfully to team members' ideas, be truthful and admit mistakes, work hard, show integrity, and ask for input from the team members. Once the leader has established these attributes and values in the team, Fisher and Sharp offer a five-step method for learning to be a lateral leader which can be applied to any project, team, or meeting. They recommend the following:

1. **Establish clear goals and objectives of the team.** Write down what the group hopes to achieve.

2. **Take the time to think systematically about the project rather than diving right in.** Gather and lay out the necessary data, analyze the data, and propose actions that are based on the analysis. As a leader, ask the appropriate questions: Do we have the information we need? What's causing the problems we're trying to solve?

3. **Learn while you're going along.** Conduct minireviews daily or weekly rather than waiting until the end of the project to see what you have learned. In this way, the team can use these midcourse conclusions to make adjustments and the data are fresh in everyone's mind.

4. **Seek out the best fit for the team members, taking into consideration the required tasks and members' interests.** Suggest writing a list of tasks and matching them to individuals or subgroups. If no one wants a particular task, brainstorm to find a way to make it more interesting or challenging. Draw out quieter members of the group.

5. **Provide feedback and praise.** Ask for their feedback. Allow them to ask questions.

Other researchers have added their suggestions:

Informal communication occurs when people talk for work reasons outside of a formal business context—talking in the corridors, business discussions by the coffee machine, all outside formal meetings. Study results show that those team members maintaining high levels of informal communication with colleagues were the most effective in obtaining the cooperation of the other team members (third parties from various departments). This research is crucial for managers who are trying to coordinate cooperation between several teams or departments. It is especially important for managers who don't have authority over team members because they don't have any tools to bring the third party in line.[11]

Star performers often don't have the power to fire anybody. They can't give out promotions, bonuses, or raises. What they have is the ability to bring people together to get things done. People want lead-ers who are knowledgeable, create energy in others, pay attention to everyone who's involved in a project—they show them they matter.[12]

One of our participants shares his thoughts:

As an ROTC officer in colleges and universities, you don't have real command over your team. The captain of an ROTC company is a twenty-one-year-old with 120 people in his or her command who are eighteen to twenty-one years old. There are the same issues as in cor-porate America: They can't hire or fire, increase or decrease wages, but they still need to get things done. Tough taskmasters aren't tough enough, so they have to figure out how to maximize the abilities that they come with. One captain had to take what was given to him. He had no opportunity to handpick his team. His solution: people skills. Understand where they're coming from. Identify and maximize skills.

RECOGNIZING THE ACCOMPLISHMENTS OF YOUR TEAM

Leaders are always aware of how they are going to reward the team to recog-nize the members' accomplishments. Popular wisdom would indicate that the reward frequently has to do with money: Raise their salary or give them a bonus and they're happy. But research often finds that money is not always the primary motivator. Recognition and appreciation are important as well.

If you show people that you appreciate them, it energizes them. Sometimes it can be just an e-mail or a thank-you note. They want to perform for you; they want to exceed their limits of what you think they can do.

ᴄⱴᴐ

My old boss was a tough taskmaster, but anyone who ever worked for him agreed that we were all willing to "fall on our swords" for him. Why? I don't know. He always expected the most from you, but you always wanted to work really hard to make him proud. You always knew that he really cared about you and recognized your hard work.

After the September 11, 2001, attack on the World Trade Center many corporate leaders were caught out of town, away from their control cen-ters. The CEO of Home Depot was no exception. When a comment was made by a television interviewer remarking on what Home Depot was contributing to the relief effort as he was driving back to Atlanta, Bob Nardelli responded publicly. "I am so proud of what my team has done. . . . You would be so impressed with what they're doing, the passion with which our associates are stepping up to contribute."

This is what leaders do—publicly recognizing the team, sharing in the pride of what the team members are doing, caring about their people. Another executive was at a conference on the West Coast, away from his New York area headquarters, and was unable to get back to the office for several days. His assistant stayed on top of airline updates and reservations and called him at 5 A.M. to let him know his morning flight was still scheduled. Upon returning, he sent an e-mail to the other members of the management team acknowledging her tenacity and sent a copy to her as well. Little things can mean a lot.

STRATEGIES AND SUGGESTIONS FOR TEAM LEADERSHIP

Here are some thoughts from our senior leaders on how they manage teams. However, they also can be applied to our earliest team-leading opportunities:

1. **First, examine the goals and reasons for developing the team.** Then begin to choose the players: Who will create the best fit? Who has the talent, the experience, the greatest potential? Who will work well together? Should you use existing people or bring in new team members? Once you have established or assessed the team makeup, set the tone: What should the team expect from you? What can you expect from them? Gauge skills and talent and start to get to know each other, building relationships.

2. **Practice making decisions.** There are different levels of decision making, the most common involving basic day-to-day issues such as, "The vendor can't deliver our marketing materials for the conference due date. What should we do?" Don't labor over the decision; just make it and go on to the next issue. Then you have the more strategic decisions: "There's a talent shortage. We need to attract more engineers to our company. What's our plan?" You want to work with your team on these decisions. Then you have the high-risk decisions at senior levels. A CEO, for example, probably makes about five or six mission-critical, life-or-death decisions a year (a merger, going public/launching an initial public offering, getting back to the core business, selling off business units). That's what they get paid for— the biggest risks, making the life-or-death decisions.

3. **In decision making you should always have two or three primary goals, priorities, or issues.** Senior managers orchestrate, set the vision for, and constantly look at the activities of their subordinates and can visualize how the activities of those staff members can fit into the two or three key issues.

4. **Focus the attention of the team to make sure that they all keep sight of the primary goals.** Part of the job of an executive is to communicate and reinforce the goals of the mission to the team. And you have to keep the team motivated during the inevitable tough times. It takes a lot of work, but it's got to be done. Always refocus team members on "how we are to achieve our goals."

5. **Motivate everyone on the team, even those who aren't going to be leaders.** It's a matter of recognizing people, making them feel that their work makes a difference or that someone knows about their contribution—even if it's just sending a two-line e-mail to thank them for their hard work/report, info, and so on.

6. **Reevaluate your thinking in terms of team success based the resources on hand.** Everyone has limits on his or her team in terms of resources. There's not enough time, enough money, enough people to complete the task.

7. **Work hard to make your mark on early projects and you will be given bigger assignments with more responsibility and visibility.** I was fortunate enough to have leadership experience at a very early point in my career. I have often taken on projects or jobs that no one else wanted. My advice? Get as much leadership experience as you can, as early as you can, even if it's outside the organization, in volunteer situations, associations, and so on.

8. **Make sure that everyone knows exactly what the task is and what you want.** Lack of planning, especially at the beginning of a project, can lead to a lot of questions, subteams going off in the wrong direction, and misunderstanding of what the team leader wants, causing time delays and frustration. Teams can be far more effective if the members receive clear direction from the beginning. "I spend 50 percent of my allotted time planning, 25 percent doing, and 25 percent evaluating," says one executive.

9. **Don't give lots of unnecessary details.** They can further confuse what you want to accomplish. First, you want to encourage independent thinking within the given guidelines. Let other people come up with interesting ways of getting the job done. You just

want the results. Second, provide some reasoning as to why you want the team to do something, but keep it concise. Don't give them a laundry list of reasons. Third, don't confuse encouragement or cheerleading with intent. Rather than vague statements, provide a strategy or specific goals.

SUMMARY

Success Secret #3: Define Your Role as a Team Leader or Participant

♦ First, examine the goals and reasons for developing the team. Then you can begin to choose the players: who will create the best fit; who has the talent, the experience, the potential; who will work well together; whether you will use existing people or bring in new team members, and so on.

♦ Identify team membership and leadership characteristics. Balance the strengths and weaknesses of team members, how they fit and work together.

♦ In a challenging, fast-paced environment team members need recognition, open lines of communication, schedules that most effectively maximize their productivity—and some time for fun.

♦ In times of crisis team leadership requires confidence and outstanding communication.

♦ Give good instructions to your team. Don't give too much direction or micromanage, consider using different communication styles, and take your time to make sure everyone understands the task.

♦ Understand that today project management—and success in those projects—is the key to career advancement.

♦ People skills and communication skills are critical to team leadership when you're not the boss.

♦ Motivate the team by recognizing team accomplishments.

For a list of research participants, please see page xvii.

Develop a Mentoring Network

෴

I think the need to have a variety of role models can't be emphasized enough. People think that one or two role models are sufficient. Some women even recognize that they need male role models. But to really develop your own management and professional identity, it is a good idea to take a little bit from as many good examples as possible.

There are few successful men—I might venture to say *no* successful men—who will tell you that they did it all on their own. They have had guidance, mentors, advocates, sponsors, and advisers to share insights, give advice, and act as role models. We found the same trend among successful women. In our last book, in which we interviewed nearly a hundred successful senior-level women, all of them stated that they have had a mentor or sponsor.

Mentors can help aspiring leaders by creating an opportunity for a less experienced individual to function in the role of an "aide" to a more senior person. It's a wonderful opportunity to become knowledgeable about business matters and decision making.

෴

You can't do it without mentors. In my experience you don't generally have too many role models, but find yourself about eight people you respect and admire and work with them. You can't be successful if you don't let yourself be mentored.

෴

Mentors are crucial to success. They give advice, identify roadblocks and barriers, serve as sounding boards, and help you think for yourself. Gender is not important.

WHAT IS A MENTOR?

When we ask people how they define a mentor, the answer is usually pretty predictable. It's someone, usually an older, more experienced person—often a boss—who "shows you the ropes," gets you noticed, and gives advice and support. But increasingly we're seeing evidence that it goes way beyond that. In our first book, *Seven Secrets of Successful Women*, we talked about the importance of having a mentor, an advocate, a coach, and 100 percent of the women we interviewed shared that opinion. Based on our subsequent research and input from our clients, I still feel the same way, only we have seen an evolution in mentoring.

At that time there was the mantra "you need a mentor, you need a mentor," so everyone ran out to find a mentor. Companies said, "Okay, let's get these mentoring programs up and running. We especially want to get women involved in the mentoring process." But at that time there was only one main model: If you were on the fast track, were early in your career, and were identified as having high potential, you probably were assigned a mentor, a "buddy," or a coach. But what about everyone else? It caused great frustration. You knew you needed a mentor, but you didn't know how to get one. Imagine the confusion: "Okay, I'm going to get a mentor. Umm, what do I do now?"

Lynn brought up an interesting point as we were discussing this issue. She commented that everyone has hopped on the bandwagon and said, "We have to get mentors." It seems that just the fact of *having* a mentor is supposed to be the accomplishment. But this is missing the point: Mentoring should be a means to an end, a *process,* not the goal in itself. It's like saying, "Okay, now I have a mentor, so I guess I'm successful."

First, it's important to get a better sense of what a mentor is. In the old days you had one person, usually a more senior man, who was seen as the "font of all knowledge." He could advise you on any organizational issue, get you noticed, get you into the right clubs, help you meet the right people, and so forth. But now we are starting to realize that no single person can do it all. You actually need several, or a number of, people who can serve in different roles for you: personal adviser, professional adviser, resource person, sponsor, counselor, support person. We asked a lot of people what mentors have done for them. Here is a partial list of mentoring roles:

+ Increase visibility
+ Teach; show you the ropes
+ Give information and advice
+ Provide sponsorship

- Encourage networks; make sure you meet the right people
- Provide feedback
- Make recommendations
- Act as an advocate or support person
- Provide legitimacy and credibility
- Act as a resource person
- Challenge you to go beyond your comfort level
- Help develop skills
- Help mentor the next generation

THE BENEFITS OF MENTORS AND MENTORING

Everyone gets different things from the mentoring experience, but several of the top executives we spoke with identified some of the best advantages to developing strong mentoring relationships.

Advice and Guidance

Mentors can provide valuable input about the corporate environment and about your particular style—your strengths and weaknesses.

I had a colleague in his late fifties, early sixties, who was in a mentoring mode. Young people, his protégés, would bring work to him, and he would give them recommendations. He would say, "I like what I see, but maybe it could be a little crisper," and the like. Very kindly. It was hard to backfire. People wanted to please him. They knew that he had their development in mind. Also, in my opinion, it's better to let people learn from their mistakes. It's better to help guide them and then let them live with the impact of their mistakes. Although you need to give them some guidance, it's a learning experience to let them dig themselves out.

∽

One thing that I have seen is the importance of women being able to work easily with men by developing an understanding of the differences between the genders and also an understanding of other women who possess more masculine characteristics (i.e., leadership style), if you want to call it that. One of the roles of a mentor, for example, may be to facilitate the understanding of differences in management style and the appropriate reaction and interaction.

Feedback

Mentors also can serve as a source of unbiased, sometimes brutally honest feedback. Take a closer look at the feedback you get from senior people. If you look at it objectively, you'll probably see some truth in what they're saying even if it's not what you want to hear.

Part of mentoring is giving good feedback. Most people have a hard time being tactfully honest with others. They're concerned that they risk destroying those relationships. Many people end up just avoiding it. But it's really a lifelong exercise that you have to take on proactively.

Sometimes people mentor you. You may not like them as a person, but they give you great information or feedback. My former boss was not a particularly likable person. Every time I would hand her my monthly reports, which I spent many hours preparing, she would always answer, "So what? Where's the benefit? How does it impact our bottom line?" After hearing that a couple of times, I made sure that I always asked myself those questions as I was writing my reports. I worked much harder on them. I hate to admit it, but she did push me to do better work.

When I was a senior manager at a large multinational company, I prided myself on the fact that I knew most of the executive team. I felt that I was very well accepted and respected for my work. But when I was talking to one of my male colleagues one day, someone who was "one of the guys" with the company leaders, he said, "You know, you have such a good sense of humor, it's a shame that most people don't see this side of you." Ironically, I knew that a sense of informality and humor was a huge part of the corporate culture there. But I thought that if people saw me as more social, I would be taken as a lightweight. What I thought was valued, my hard work and professionalism, was only one piece of the puzzle. It was really helpful to have a different perspective on how others perceive you.

Challenge

Mentors can help when you're faced with a new career challenge. If you rise to the challenge and do good work in a demanding situation, that reflects well on you. Performance is key, and people *will* notice.

I've been given a number of promotions in my career that were a stretch, but my bosses always stayed involved to support me. They didn't want me to fail, not only for my sake but for their own as well. This mutual trust allows both the young leader and the sponsor to feel comfortable in testing leadership skills in slightly riskier opportunities.

 oνɔ

I had the chance to develop early leadership experience when my boss gave me an opportunity to manage a corporate department in a discipline that was totally new for me. The experience taught me that it was my management skills that were important and that I could transfer them to different areas of the organization and be successful in spite of a low level of technical knowledge of the area I was assigned to manage. That was a terrific growth experience.

oνɔ

If you find someone who seems to have potential, set high standards and push hard. Then stand back and see what happens. If they haven't had a lot of opportunities, let them step up to the plate.

oνɔ

When Henry Kissinger's staff would bring him reports, he would tell them two or three times, "No, it's not good enough. No, still not good enough."—but without even looking at the reports! Then, the third or fourth time, he would finally say, "Okay, now I'll read it."

Helping You Mentor the Next Generation

Being a good mentor gives you the skills to one day be a good leader for others in the organization.

I would encourage women to take on more mentoring opportunities. I say often that "no one moves ahead unless they're adequately mentored." I have heard in meetings almost a denial that people have been mentored, but I know that they really have been; they just haven't thought about it in a specific sense. But when you mentor the next generation, you improve not only that generation but also yourself.

oνɔ

I'm a great advocate of mentoring. My credo is, "Don't worry about your own career, worry about others' careers." I recall a situation, after having received my law degree, where I was suddenly promoted two levels over a number of colleagues. One of the more senior team members let me know that I was "ticking off" my former peers. The advice I was given? "You're not looking back to reach out and bring these guys along. When you're in a group setting, make sure to compliment the accomplishments of your colleagues." My first reaction was, "Why should I? They've had the same opportunities I've had." I did, however, take the advice and at the next meeting said, "John X did an excellent job on. . . ." I noticed that the group was instantly electrified. I realized that there was no downside to crediting the accomplishments of others. It always works to your advantage.

ᴄᴧᴐ

Earlier in my career my former boss advised me to consciously develop skills and seek out experiences that I could draw upon later in a leadership role. Since then I have always tried to learn something in every job situation and from every person I have ever worked with.

FINDING A MENTOR OR COACH

Many people, especially women, ask us how to find a mentor. When we do programs on mentoring strategies, we ask how many people in the audience have a mentor. Interestingly, usually no more than about a third of the participants raise their hands. The comment that we often hear is: "I keep hearing that successful people have mentors, but I don't. Does that mean that I'm not going to make it?"

Our answer is probably not what you would think. Yes, it is true that successful people generally have mentors, and I do mean that in the plural—mentors. And yes, it is possible to be successful without a mentor—it just takes a lot more time and effort. But for most people—and that means the majority of people who are not identified as having high potential and who probably will *not* be assigned a mentor—it's too overwhelming to undertake the task of "getting a mentor." They don't know where to start, whom to ask, what they need the mentor for, what they're supposed to do, and so it just doesn't get done. However, I think that the more important question is, What exactly do you think a mentor is? If you looked at the material above about the roles of a mentor, you probably realize that it really would be impossible for one person to fill the bill. More realistically, we and many other researchers advocate finding a number of people to fulfill your different mentoring needs. The question becomes not, "How can I find a mentor?" but rather, "What are my mentoring needs right now?" Then you can begin the task of identifying—and building relationships with—the people who can fill those needs. We always emphatically add that this is a two-way street. It's not only "Who can help me?" but also "Whom can I help?" We will talk about "reverse mentoring" in a minute.

Okay, so we start with the question, What do I want a mentor for? How is he or she going to help me? What do I need to learn, to develop, to share? How can I help others? Again, keep in mind that a mentor should be a means to an end, which for most people is having a more successful, rewarding work life.

Let's start with what your mentoring needs are. When we do programs on mentoring, we ask the participants to think about some of the areas in which they could use some advice, some guidance, and some information.

♦ Are you new to your job, organization, or industry and need basic information?

♦ Do you want some advice on the next step in your career advancement plan?

♦ Do you need a support person for a personal issue or a senior sponsor who can increase your visibility at work?

♦ Have you been in your job for a while? Then you probably need less informational guidance and more "next step" advice. If you are fairly senior in your field, you may need specific advice on the role of the executive: working with corporate boards, dealing with shareholders, making presentations to the media. Don't forget that reaching a senior level doesn't mean that you don't need a mentor—even new CEOs do.

Here are the experiences of several of our participants:

Three out of my seven supervisors in my professional career have been women. I don't see any difference between men and women when it comes to leadership skills. Two women particularly influenced me. One focused more on internal issues in a constructive, supportive way, things like here are the objectives and here's how to get them done. She also taught me a lot about how to manage people. The other focused more on external skills. From a marketing perspective, she taught me how to build the business and how to get and manage clients. I am now coaching two women about two levels below mine. One has about seventy people reporting to her. When we discuss where she wants to be in three to five years, I think that she could do her boss's job, which has a staff of about 650 people.

⌒⌒

Sometimes, women (and men, too) don't put forth the self-confidence that they can do a job even when their coaches/superiors feel that they can do it well.

༄

"I currently coach a thirty-four-year-old female CEO for two hours every two weeks. We talk about all kinds of things that she will need, such as running board meetings. It's a mutually positive relationship, and I believe that she would add that I have increased her productivity." When I asked this participant how he came to mentor her, he said that a colleague introduced them and thought that it would be a good match and that his skills would complement her experience.

Sometimes mentoring can be a leadership opportunity, as shown in the following story:

I have on my staff a female supervisor who generated great ideas for individuals and the work group but needed to learn how to generalize those ideas to affect a broader organizational target. She had a wonderful understanding of people, their motivations, and how to network. She provided mentorship even when no formal mentorship program existed. However, she did not see herself as a "leader" or aspire to "lead the organization." She often defaulted to a behind-the-scenes role.

I studied her natural affinity for mentoring and attempted to "reflect" it in how I positioned her and interacted with her. I consolidated two work groups under her, requiring her to learn a more strategic, less "hands-on" or "participative" style. That also caused her to have to deal with a broader, more senior stakeholder universe.

Her peoplecentric interests now play out more broadly in the organization. She now opens learning paths for many teams and expresses value throughout the organization. What she once did with individuals, she now does across the company. She seems to be at ease with her new leadership position, and senior leaders are recognizing her as a collaborative consultant on improving our company culture. She has become a "strategic leader."

What Would You Look for in a Coach/Mentor at This Point in Your Career?

You may want to keep the following needs in mind when you're starting the process of finding a mentor because you know that in most cases mentors probably are *not* going to find you. You may want to refer to the list earlier in this chapter of the roles of a mentor/advocate/support person. See how they fit into the categories below and what your needs for a mentor are. Mentors can fill the following roles:

♦ **A source of job-specific or career-specific information:** career moves, new projects you should take on, skills required, international opportunities, advice about education, and so on

♦ **An advocate to the executive or senior management team** so that you can be considered for a promotion to the next level, to new department/division leadership, or to a highly visible team, project, or committee leadership

♦ **A support person** sharing his or her experiences, successes, failures, and learning experiences when you face barriers and roadblocks

♦ **An access person to key decision makers,** helping you develop an effective network

♦ **A career sponsor:** someone to help you navigate your specific career plan

♦ **Someone to provide advice or feedback on content-specific or issue-specific areas:** project planning, software problems, succession planning, doing a budget, performance improvement, resolving staff issues, improving communication, negotiation, advice on writing a critical but sensitive letter to a client, and so on

♦ **Someone to provide an unbiased evaluation of your skills, potential, and management style** with suggestions for improvement

♦ **A source of information on how to gain greater visibility:** which are the best projects, teams, and committees to lead; what are the appropriate professional associations and volunteer opportunities to be affiliated with; where you can find information on effective networks

If you do this exercise with some colleagues or friends, you may find it interesting that most of you probably have different goals and needs in your careers. Once you have gotten a sense of what your role and responsibilities are, you will progress through a series of mentoring needs—perhaps early management issues, then team leading, and then the possible promotions and increased responsibilities. Each change in your career status may necessitate different or additional mentoring needs. And as we have discussed, you can have multiple mentors who fill several different roles.

Approaching Potential Mentors

The question we hear a lot is, How can one approach these potential mentors? A less formal approach to mentoring, that is, not depending on a formal assigned mentoring program, allows a protégé to approach a potential mentor in a different way without having the usual time commitment necessary for formal pairings. Protégés often can approach a potential mentor (of course, depending on the situation) and say something like, "I met you at a recent workshop, and I loved what you had to say about international marketing. I'm thinking about getting into that area and wondered if I could talk to you briefly about what you would recommend to broaden my area of expertise. Could I schedule perhaps half an hour at your convenience?"

First, you have indicated that you already have met. You probably have been able to assess whether this person will be receptive. If the person is not, find someone else who is. Next, you aren't asking for a lifelong commitment, just thirty minutes, and even the busiest managers usually will find time for a brown-bag lunch or a similar opportunity. One of two things will happen. Either you will get your information, which is great, or you will hit it off and perhaps be able to build a more extensive professional rapport. Either way, you are a winner.

One of the most influential people in getting me started on the right track was a woman I met only twice. I haven't seen her in years, and I'm not even sure that she would remember me. When I first started taking my doctoral courses, I had met a very impressive consultant to my college. She already had her Ph.D., and I called her to ask what she would recommend that I take as additional electives. She suggested taking as many business courses as I could, something I had never really thought about before. I thanked her and did as she recommended. I discovered that I really enjoyed the courses and had a natural affinity for management. I didn't speak to her after that, but she really made my career direction take a dramatic turn for the better.

Another option, as we mentioned above, is to be more proactive about developing your network. This is where many people have developed additional mentoring relationships. You generally will have something in common to begin with, and it will allow you to interact with more senior or experienced people with whom you would rarely have the opportunity to interact in your day-to-day work life.

In addition, tap your existing network. If you ask around, there's bound to be someone who has access to the person you want to meet. Seek and ye shall find. In any situation you can ask yourself these more tactical questions:

- Based on your indicated needs, how would you describe the components of an ideal mentoring relationship or relationships?
- Who would the mentor(s) be (their relationship, position, internal, external)?
- What should be their qualifications, skills, and background?
- How should you approach them?

New Definition of a Mentor/Coach: What It Is and How It Works

Depending on your situation, in addition to having traditional mentors, you may often have several more informal mentoring relationships, both personal and professional advisers who provide guidance in a variety of areas, possibly different mentors for different needs.

- This can require less of a time commitment for mentors, something that often precluded individuals from volunteering as a mentor in the past.
- It can be easier for a protégé to approach a potential mentor, since the protégé is not necessarily asking for a "lifelong commitment" but occasional advice, guidance, and information.
- It allows the protégé to ask for feedback from the mentor or advocate in a trusting relationship. They can discuss what the protégé may be lacking (experience, education, public speaking skills, business background) in a positive environment.
- It provides another alternative for women, since the traditional model of an assigned mentor or coach is not generally as effective for women as it is for men.
- It provides an opportunity to ask mentors/coaches for additional responsibilities as appropriate, for example, financial experience or team leadership.
- It allows a manager to provide resources and information to staff members to allow them to develop (journals, articles, online sites, professional associations, etc.).

If you take the new approach to mentoring, you will realize that there can be many aspects of the process. Yes, you can have formal mentors or sponsors with whom you meet regularly, gain insights, learn skills and strategies, gain visibility and credibility, and so on. However, you also will be able to utilize—and provide—more basic information or services. For example, I have one friend who calls every once in a while to get feedback or advice on a critical e-mail he is sending to the chief executive officer, to a colleague, to a client, to a difficult employee—"How does this sound? Does this sound too inflammatory? Do you have a good analogy for this? Do you have a good humorous story to start this out?" Am I mentoring him? Not in the strictest sense of the word, of course, but I am certainly providing a resource which forms part of his mentoring network. He describes our mentoring situation this way: "It's like on *Who Wants to be a Millionaire?*—sometimes you just need another perspective, your 'life-lines.' " I guess I'm one of his lifelines, a resource he has available if he's "stuck" on a certain problem. It works out great for us.

Another friend called me after she was offered a hugely visible, newly created job, one that wasn't in her division or realm of expertise. She was understandably apprehensive about the move, and so we talked for about an hour and a half. I told her that she would be fantastic for the position and reminded her of all the skills she brought to the job. At the end of the phone call she said, "I feel so much better. I'm really excited about taking this new job!" She did and of course did magnificently. Was I mentoring her? No, I was just giving advice, feedback, and encouragement. But in the same way that networks exist on many levels, so do mentoring opportunities. Here's another perspective:

I have five or six people who give me different things. I don't rely on one mentor, and taken together I know I can get the advice, listening, and cocounseling I need, when I need it.

Don't get hung up on a formal definition of mentoring—make it work for you. It could be ten minutes by phone twice a year. It could be more face-to-face time when you need it, for example, in a new role or dealing with a specific problem. Be brave—go find people who are respected and ask them if they can help you. They may say no, but in my experience, people are pleased to be asked. I mentor around ten to twenty people at any one time, and with each of them we contract at the start as to what I can give, what they need, and how it will work at the start so that expectations are managed well.

DEVELOPING A MENTORING NETWORK

After you asked yourself the question, "What do I want in a mentor at this point in my career?" you probably found that there are several people—or more—who need to be in your mentoring network. Many people already have some people in this network, depending on the category. For basic information or support issues, your network is probably pretty comprehensive. Perhaps you just need a more specialized one. For example, if you have experienced a dramatic life event, talking to others who have experienced the same situation can be especially helpful. Areas such as work-life balance for a new parent and a support network dealing with divorce, illness, or grief can be identified to manage a specific issue.

By contrast, if you are looking to identify senior leaders in your organization to help you navigate your career, it's obviously going to take a lot more work—and time. In this case you may want to talk with colleagues at your level or slightly above or your boss, if appropriate, about your career. Identify your goals and begin working on a strategy to identify those who will be most informative and influential. Someone you know always knows someone else at a higher level or in a different department or area of your work or knows someone else in your industry. Talk to people you trust about your goals. Ask if your trusted colleagues or friends can set up an informal informational meeting or perhaps a lunch to meet the more senior or well-connected person. But remember, it will take time to develop a relationship with this new person. You can't just say, "Hi, my name's Donna. How about hiring me for that great new job?" It can take months, so start early.

Likewise, you can ask mentors or advocates to see what professional associations or other appropriate groups you should join to come into contact with the people who can help you. Even volunteer opportunities can be doubly beneficial; you're helping others and maybe yourself as well. Be prepared to return the favor to those who help you out. It really helps to start planning your needs in advance. We're talking about mentoring relationships here. You want to establish open communication, trust, and a mutually advantageous relationship. That won't happen overnight.

Don't assume that women make better mentors for other women. Many of the successful women we interviewed stated that they had male mentors. There weren't any senior women for most of them when they were starting out. The important issue is developing a relationship that's a good fit, not necessarily the gender.

As we have discussed in our research, author Kathy Kram identifies mentoring as a network of resources or potential resources. These are alliances both for career and for personal growth and development.[1] She identifies two categories or functions of mentoring development: career functions and psychosocial functions. First, there are the career functions, for example, learning the ropes and preparing for advancement at work. The other is psychosocial: developing the individual's sense of competence, identity, and effectiveness. Mentoring relationships may fulfill one or both of these functions.

The career functions include sponsorship, or opening doors to the right opportunities; coaching (teaching, providing feedback); protection (support, a buffer); exposure (opportunities for visibility); and challenge (providing stretch assignments).

As part of the psychosocial functions, mentors potentially can provide a role model (demonstrating appropriate behaviors, attitudes, and values), counseling (a forum for discussing personal and/or professional issues), acceptance and confirmation (support and respect), and friendship (caring and sharing).

This is an interesting premise, especially since we often have been asked about the difference between a sponsor and a mentor. Although there are several assumptions, it is safe to assume that sponsorship applies primarily to the workplace, that is, facilitating the advancement of one's career. Of course, this can be done using a variety of aspects of mentoring: increasing visibility, gaining increased credibility or legitimacy, and facilitating stretch assignments to provide leadership opportunities. Mentors, in contrast, while certainly often serving in this capacity, can do much more. They can be a sounding board and a support person—sharing their experiences and giving advice, feedback, and reassurance. They can provide personal as well as professional insights or advice—a friend.

The reporter David Foote comments on the factors that influence a leader's success by reminiscing about a graduate business school project involving CEO interviews.

There was precious little clear consensus, except in one area: mentors and coaches. Nearly every leader mentioned that such relationships at various career stages had much to do with his development and ultimate success. We discovered that these influential teachers often were not their direct superiors, but someone else who took an interest in them and provided feedback and counsel. While early successes may have helped some to be "discovered," these CEOs insisted that the more significant factor was that their employers encouraged mentoring, coaching, and the skills development to support them.[2]

REVERSE MENTORING

A genuine leader-teacher absorbs as much information from the learner as the learner does from the teacher. So, if you're not teaching others, you're missing out on the chance to learn from them.[3]

I'm not going to take credit for this term. Jack Welch, former CEO of General Electric (GE), coined the phrase, but I have been writing and talking about it for years. When I ask workshop participants how they envision a mentor or mentors, they usually say, "Someone older, more senior, wiser, and more experienced." But in my opinion that's the old model. It is based on the assumption of a linear career path: You perform, you get a promotion, you get experience, you get a promotion. . . . However, think about your workplace. Many of you have teams, cross-functional work environments, older bosses, younger bosses, women, men, and different cultures, races, and points of reference. It's impossible to generalize.

This is especially evident in a technology environment. Fast-paced, innovative, crazed, outside-the-box thinking . . . how can you tell who is mentoring whom? It's whoever is the expert in that particular area, and it changes constantly. The "resident expert" in today's meeting is taking notes in the next one. It's fluid. Of course, there will always be a certain degree of content expertise, but this is a cross-functional environment of many perspectives and points of view.

Let's say that your organization or division has realized that it's a bit behind in technology. Sure, there's an information technology (IT) person, but is he or she operating in a silo or is that person an integral part of the operational team? Jack Welch came to this same observation several years ago. Some of his top executives were less concerned with technology, and he planned to do something about it. He called upon the young, technologically savvy employees at GE to get them back on track.

Jack Welch initiated a program which he called "reverse mentoring." Believing that his most senior staff needed to learn more about how technology could be used more effectively at GE, he assigned his top 600 managers to find a mentor—someone who was younger than they were and technologically savvy. (And who was going to say no to Jack Welch?) Presidents of divisions, senior vice presidents and the like, some of whom were admittedly less than proficient in technology applications, sought out their new coaches. Twenty-something techies were suddenly the teachers, senior leaders, their students.

The results were immediate. Senior managers with little technology experience were ordering items online—"I ordered a gift for my wife on the Internet!" Others who were already technologically aware shared stories of examining competitors' websites to discover user deficiencies in their competitors' services—"Ok, we can do this for our customers online and they can't—we can market that advantage." Conversely, the younger "mentors" cite important opportunities in which their "students" talk about how they do things, how they make decisions, talk about their experiences. A great opportunity for each generation.[4]

Like the participants at GE, I have talked to a number of young people who have mentored more senior people. They discussed the various stages they experienced in their mentoring relationships—getting to know each other, building a rapport, finding out about each other, discovering things in common. The more junior person can also give his or her technical expertise and a fresh perspective on the way things are done.

The more senior person gives the protégé advice, support, and guidance and shows him or her the ropes while providing insight into behaviors, attitudes, competencies, and the like. The mentor or advocate creates opportunities in which the protégé can become more visible and gives him or her challenging or high-visibility assignments.

One of our participants shared his insights:

Everyone can be a potential role model if they do something well that you would like to emulate. I have one person who is a role model for me (actually she is junior to me) simply for the way she writes memos and other communications. Her writing style has just the right tone of professionalism but also just the right amount of relational content that achieves a great balance. I usually put in too much of one or the other, and usually at the wrong time. I really admire her writing and use her as a role model for myself.

WOMEN AND MENTORING

A number of our corporate colleagues have commented, "In the past five years or so we've started formal mentoring opportunities and initiatives, especially for women and minorities, but we haven't had the success that we anticipated. What do you think is the problem?" One of the problems is the assumption that a formal mentoring program is the key. Traditionally, many formal mentoring programs relied on assigned mentor-protégé teams, "creating" a mentoring relationship. In the past these formal programs paired young men with more senior men, who often saw themselves in their younger protégés. They went to lunch, played golf and racquetball, and so forth. It was the continuation of the old boys' network. And since it's human nature to have a natural affinity for like-minded people, many women didn't fit the traditional mold. Many of the women we spoke to were not particularly comfortable in those relationships; there wasn't a good fit. Their mentors didn't have much insight into their particular situation or needs. Some women, however, thought that their mentors were fantastic; in assigned mentoring initiatives it can often be just the luck of the draw.

But some of the more recent research indicates that women do not fare as well in formal, assigned mentoring programs as men do. Likewise, women—and, I will add, men—may benefit more from a more informal model based on complementary participants with mutual interests and attitudes.

Is there an area that I think may allow women to improve their career success and advancement? Include more men in mentor-mentee relationships and in networks. Spend less energy identifying negative male behaviors and more energy collaborating with male colleagues who "get it."

But still, it is enormously helpful to have one or more advocates or sponsors to fill a wide range of needs. Here's an example:

A talented and experienced editor recounted that after a morning strategy meeting her male boss and a couple of male colleagues headed into the men's room, talking and laughing—you know, the male-bonding thing. She went back to her office to get some work done over lunch. A couple of hours later the group of men came wandering in from a pleasant lunch, at which they probably continued discussing the strategies from the morning meeting. She felt clearly left out of the process. She thought, When the heck did they decide to go out to lunch? And why didn't they invite me along? Then it occurred to her—aha, it was in the men's room!

We talked about the situation later and came up with a couple of solutions for the future—as many of us know, this will happen again. First, we need to develop relationships with the key players. This may take time, of course, but it is enormously helpful to have someone looking out for our career development and visibility. When this type of situation happens again, he or she will be sure to think, Oh, some of us are going out to lunch. I'll go see if Jane wants to join us.

The second thing we agreed about in this scenario is that Jane automatically went back to her office to work through lunch. If you ask many women, they will tell you that they frequently work through lunch because they have so much to do. However—and this is a huge generalization, of course—many men make it a point to have lunch with colleagues or clients. They know the value of networking, visibility, building relationships, having colleagues and bosses see them in a different light, discussing nonbusiness issues, and learning about colleagues' varied interests and accomplishments in an informal setting. It goes back to a common issue:

Many women think everyone will know they're working hard when they work through lunch. The truth is that they don't. If you're not out there with the others, they don't see you.

What Did Some of the Senior Women We Interviewed Say about Their Mentoring Experiences?

My mentor told me earlier in my career to relax a little in my management style. He said, "Don't worry, you're doing fine." I think I'm still pretty tough as a manager, but now I am more willing to let my feminine side show. I haven't been on specific committees for the advancement for women, but I have been very involved in the growth of my own employees—both women and men. I have tried to guide "street-tough" employees and have encouraged education; for example, we had a celebration for an employee who just received her GED. I think that mentors are good for women, not only nurturing ones but the "kick-in-the-butt" ones too.

೩

The president originally didn't want to promote me to this position— he was hesitant because I was a woman. However, my boss, a man, said that he would change the president's mind—"Just give me a little time. . . ." Six months later I got the job. My boss helped me "fix" the situation by intervening and promoting my visibility. The president had to get used to the idea of a woman in that position.

೩

It's still a man's world. It's very helpful to get a perspective from a man.

೩

My mentor was the company chairman. I admire the way he works—he handles crises that come up, then moves from priority to priority quickly. He has taught me how to manage my time and prioritize. He doesn't work late and has few meetings. But I have one role model for managing time and another one for managing people.

೩

One of my mentors asked me, "What exactly are you going to be doing in five years?" He was a "kick-in-the-butt" type, which I guess we all need sometimes. But he really got me to think about it.

೩

I've mentored a lot of people in my career—often five to six at a time. I have promoted a lot of women and am very sympathetic to child-care issues for women and men, especially since the birth of my son.

◈

I was told by my former [male] boss, a good friend, "You know, I could never go out to lunch or dinner with you—just you—in the same way I can with another male executive." He was right. People could have jumped to conclusions.

◈

I think that women need to help promote other women. A colleague of mine, a guy, said that he would like to recommend more women for his department—he had a vice-presidential position open, for example, but he couldn't think of any qualified women to interview. I said, "If I can get you a list, would you at least consider interviewing some women?" The next day I gave him a list of twenty qualified women, and he ended up hiring one of them. I think that women need to be advocates for other women and raise their awareness. But I think that I am a role model not only for women but for men as well.

SUMMARY

Success Secret #4: Develop a Mentoring Network

♦ Select several mentors; however, it doesn't matter if the mentor is a man or woman. Look for mentors who fill different roles or offer different perspectives. Sometimes we need nurturing mentors, sometimes informational or guidance mentors, and sometimes "kick-in-the-butt" mentors.

♦ Ask yourself why you need specific mentors. Who can help you with your career goals? Having a mentor is the means to an end, not the goal itself. And don't forget to mentor others.

♦ Develop a mentoring network: Find mentors through networks, both internal and external, personal and professional, formal and informal.

♦ Look for mentors everywhere, not just in positions senior to your own. Mentors may be more junior; it depends on who has the expertise that you want to learn.

For a list of research participants, please see page xvii.

Build Effective Networks

ฝ

Women are great when it comes to achieving results in their own groups, but many keep their heads down and don't look beyond the team. It's imperative to network outside the area you work in. That's how things get done in an organization.

*N*etworking is a term which is becoming somewhat overused and "under-understood," in my opinion. Most people think of networking in a strict sense—when they're looking for a new job: "Hmmm, let me see who I can call. . . ." But there's so much more to a network. Networks can and should be used for a variety of reasons.

- ♦ What if you need advice on handling a difficult employee—or boss?
- ♦ What if you're starting a new project for your department or organization? Has someone you know done the same thing somewhere else?
- ♦ What if you're interested in pursuing an international assignment or making a change to another division?
- ♦ What if you are new to the organization or would like to gain visibility with more senior managers?
- ♦ What if you want to start a volunteer project for your team?
- ♦ What if you're planning to go on parental leave and want to talk to others who have done that?

What does it take to develop a network? When we did the research for our first book a few years ago, there was a consensus that "women need to network." But at that time I believe that it was mistakenly seen as a *goal* for many people (as it sometimes can be with mentoring)—"I want to have a huge network." Okay, but what do you want it for? How can it help you? How can you help others? How does it work? We see now that networking should be a means to an end, not the end in itself. Having a large group of contacts doesn't do anything for you if it doesn't have a purpose and it's not nurtured and shared. How does it make you do your job better? How does it make you more productive? How does it give you more balance and meaning in your life?

First, you want to determine the reason for your network, the goal—what you want to do. Then you can think about how the people in the network can help you (or perhaps how you can help them). Do you want to gain visibility with, or access to, more senior managers? Do you want to share information with others? Do you want advice? Do you need a support network? Do you want to develop a social network outside of work? Do you want an opportunity to bounce ideas off colleagues? Do you want to develop a network to help gain balance or creativity or spirituality in your life? We need to focus on what we want a network to do for us—and how we can use it to help others.

If you want to be better at networking, start by recognizing what you don't know but need to know. Then figure out who can supply that knowledge—and cultivate relationships with those people. . . . Understand the economics of networking. Networking is a barter system. You need an expertise to trade—something others need, but don't have. Be prepared to help out a lot of people before asking for anything in return. You start with a negative trade balance and build up credits over time.[1]

When I conduct workshops on networking, I often do an exercise that asks people to focus on their networking needs at *this stage* of their lives. Those needs change. What you need or want now in a network is not necessarily what you will need in a year or two. You need to develop and update your networks continuously. Ask yourself, Of these possible areas, are there one or two that struck a chord? Perhaps you see yourself in one of the following situations:

♦ **You are early in your career and looking for advice and direction.** What assignments or projects should you apply for? How can you get leadership experience? Should you go back to school to advance?

♦ **You have been at your firm for a few years but now realize that you need to start networking with more senior managers for advice and**

support. You realize that you need to have a sponsor, but where should you begin?

♦ **You wish to gain more visibility with key people at the organization or with your customers.** You work really hard, but no one seems to know it. How can you get someone to help you become more visible?

♦ **You want to develop your social or fitness-minded network and have a little more fun in your life.** Since you work long hours, how can you accomplish this? Who can give you advice about this?

♦ **As you have risen in your career, you have found that you need more meaning or balance in your life to counteract your stressful environment.** What have other people in the same situation done to create balance in their lives? Are there volunteer opportunities that may suit your interests and lifestyle? Are there organizations that you may want to join?

♦ **You have had an event, situation, or crisis in your life.** How can you develop a support network for issues such as parenting, coping with divorce, health and wellness, work-life balance, and midlife crises?

When you narrow your networking needs to one or two areas, it can really help you focus on the "how to" of developing your network.

COMMUNITIES OF PRACTICE

"Communities of practice" is a cool name for groups of like-minded people who get together to share . . . well, whatever they want to share. It can be social, organizational, professional, or informational—the possibilities are limitless. Let's say you have an interest in learning to ski, or paint, or speak French, or you want to join a support group, or volunteerism appeals to you. How do you start? Ask people at work. Ask others who are already involved in that activity. Look online. Contact various associations. Call the nearest office of a charity or another volunteer group. Become a member of a house of worship. Or you could start your own group. In one corporation a group of women decided to create their own network that could address their specific needs.

> *When progress for women at [our firm] wasn't happening as quickly as many of us would have liked, the women partners banded together and created our own annual meeting. Then we invited the firm's top executives to listen to our concerns, to discuss issues, and to work on solutions.*[2]

Another large corporate program offered a different perspective. When we were doing a seminar, we asked the participants about positive networking experiences they had had. One person mentioned the Valley Forge Ski Club, and at least a quarter of the people there said, "Oh, I belong to that. It's a great place to meet fun people." Individuals frequently seek out their own communities of practice. A colleague of mine was very interested in doing volunteer work with Native Americans, and so she joined a group and spent a week working on a reservation in Arizona. They had a great time and did some terrific work.

That's something that we have seen a huge increase in: the importance of volunteerism in organizations, something that is often modeled by the most senior management. We have talked about technology millionaires donating their time and money to worthwhile causes. Senator Bill Frist of Tennessee, a surgeon, chooses to spend some of his recess time from Congress performing highly specialized surgeries with a team of physicians in developing countries.

Sometimes interesting outcomes are possible. For example, in one corporate program I did, one of the participants shared her interest in Habitat for Humanity. She thought it provided a great opportunity to develop her skills, help other people, and work with people with similar interests. Interestingly, on the other side of the room a very senior manager raised her hand and said to the much more junior person, "At the break, could I talk to you? I've been wanting to get involved in Habitat for Humanity myself." One thing struck me immediately. Remember when we talked about "reverse mentoring" in Chapter 4? Think about it. Who is the "expert" in this case? Not the more senior person. Not only did this become a conversation between two people with similar interests, it became a possible opportunity for the more junior person to develop a relationship with the much more senior person.

Women know how to network. They do it all the time to build relationships. However, many of them know that they need to network more—and more effectively. A research study shows one perspective:

Men and women differ in networking skills—men spend more time networking to further business goals. Men integrate business into their social lives more.[3]

However, many women complain—rightfully—that more often than not, higher-level networking, where most of the deals are made, is done on the golf course. Although many women are taking up golf, this can still be a challenge.

We are beginning to hear about changes in networking opportunities, some alternatives. We have seen a lot of options available for networking. One group of female chief executive officers (CEOs) in high-tech companies get together for potluck suppers; they talk about business strategy, getting venture capital, and working with corporate boards as well as the other things "women talk about." Another group of 200 of the most senior and respected women in corporations met for a weekend spa retreat at the Breakers. Not only did they discuss how to get more women on corporate boards and how to make presentations to national media, shareholders, and financial analysts, they had massages and facials and enjoyed getting together with women in similar situations. Outward Bound types of activities are also popular. Although used more for team building than for networking, these frequently gender-blind, "no one is an expert" activities provide an outstanding opportunity to get to know people in a far different light than you could at work, which is great for developing relationships. Lynn has done several of these programs in different countries. She said that they really do facilitate relationship development, especially across cultures, which can often be more challenging. (And no, there are lots of variations. You don't always have to rappel down a mountain or jump from the top of fifty-foot pole.)

Here are some other insights on networking:

It's not like the old days where vice presidents called each other up to play golf and make decisions. Now the way to make a sale or influence a high-impact decision is to build, nurture, and mobilize a vast network of key influencers at every level and in every function of the operation.[4]

∽

Men network in sports, and that sometimes is a challenge for women—they have to try to make sure that this isn't a disadvantage. I've worked on my own networking, but, for example, I don't golf. Others have suggested that I take it up. (I'm an avid mountain climber. I just came back from a climb of Mount Everest with my four-teen-year-old. Not much networking there.) What do I do instead? I spend a lot of time just getting together and having coffee with people, pockets of time in an unstructured agenda. I put my feet up and chat for a while. It's important to be social in the environment.

∽

There are some serious management players whose networks are a huge part of what they offer to their business, whether as external consultants or internal hotshot hirings. We're not talking about the ability to throw a smart party, but about the ability to identify the knowledge, skills and influence that individuals and groups outside the business have to offer, how they interrelate and how the organization can tap into them.[5]

USING TECHNOLOGY IN NETWORKING

We're seeing a lot more examples of virtual networking these days. One example: Adventure teams—high-level, high-risk extreme teams—sometimes are made up of international members who have never met each other before. How do these teams get together? In one case the team started its networking on the Internet. Team Eco-Internet founders Ian Adamson and Robert Nagle met virtually in 1994. A year later they founded the team. Now Team Eco-Internet includes an American software developer, an Australian entrepreneur, an American firefighter, and a window washer from New Zealand among its eight world-class athletes from all over the world.[6]

Younger people especially zero in on the unique capabilities of virtual networking. Here are some examples of pre-MBA (master of business administration) students using technology to their networking advantage:

♦ Nine incoming Wharton MBAs climb aboard a U-Haul truck and head off to IKEA in Philadelphia for furniture and housewares for their new dorms and apartments. What's unusual about that? They arranged the trip via an international virtual call on the Internet before they even arrived in Philadelphia.

♦ A dozen incoming MBA students at the University of Michigan hike the Inca Trail near Machu Pichu on an adventure trip organized on the Web and led by a second-year Michigan student—all before they even start school in the fall.

♦ A group of pre-MBAs at Harvard starts to collaborate on a book about admissions strategies for the business school admissions process—again, before classes even begin.

♦ Nearly fifty incoming Harvard students from Silicon Valley start a discussion group on Yahoo! and organize golf games, barbecues, and other outings for when they reach Cambridge in the fall.

♦ Stanford MBA students are given access to a password-protected Web site once they have been accepted into the program. Even before they start classes, students plan happy hours "from Hong Kong to Buenos

Aires and arrange to share truck rentals for the trip from the Midwest to Palo Alto."

♦ Three Lebanese students from France, Kuwait, and Canada, all heading to Wharton in the fall, decide to meet in Lebanon in June by posting details about their backgrounds on Wharton's Web site. They find friends and even relatives in common and get to know each other before they start school.[7]

What are these young people doing that the rest of us are not? They're using technology more than ever before, and they realize that networking can be a virtual, no-boundaries environment. Be honest. When I said "networking," how many of you thought of it as "face-to-face" events: conferences, golf outings, professional association happy hours? Well, of course they are. But consider some of the possibilities above—this is another important aspect of networking. Think of why you want to network. You want advice, guidance, solutions to problems, more social or fitness activities, volunteer opportunities, support, information. . . . Not only can most of these things be organized online, many of them can be done online.

Those of us with international networks may never have met the people we communicate with regularly. Online chatrooms for advice? They are often faceless, even nameless people who can share information with us. New to a company? In a remote office? Technology is a great way to make connections and build up one's internal network. Want to know what other companies in your industry are doing? Want to "meet" your counterparts who are doing what you're doing to share stories and compare notes? Start your own bulletin board or chatroom. Just a few years ago, when we asked our program participants to brainstorm about networks that had worked well for them, almost no one mentioned virtual networks. In fact, even now I still don't hear that response from many corporate types. However, when you ask younger people the same question, it's a totally different story. It's a way of life. We need to start thinking about how we can use technology to improve our networks.

Business Week magazine sponsors an extensive "Business School Forum" in which prospective business school students can begin their virtual dialogues on every topic under the sun, from debating which schools are better to what kind of GMAT scores can get you into certain schools. At an impartial site like this, usage is heavy and lively. Ironically, several schools tried to copy the successful *Business Week* model and set up their own preadmission sites. However, those sites never really took off. The students were aware that the admissions department "Big Brother" was reading what they were discussing. The dialogue was much less lively. However, once students were admitted, password-protected sites were provided for them and the dialogue was animated and informative.[8] And once you have completed your time at school? An interesting statistic: Fully 80 percent of Harvard Business School alumni find jobs through networking. Who says networking doesn't work?

Can organizations provide this kind of password-protected environment in which employees can share thoughts and insights? Is it viable? Is it advisable? Can it really remain anonymous? Or is it something that could be set up by professional associations or industry members? These are some interesting thoughts to pursue.

Also using technology, Eileen Luhta McFarlane, senior business analyst at EDS, has found a winning formula for career success as a telecommuter, having been promoted twice in the last two years. She regularly checks during work projects that she is meeting the sales teams' needs. Afterward, she asks whether they would recommend her to others within EDS. This is all part of her strategy to become more visible there. "Constant feedback is especially important when you're working virtually," she says. A strong networker, she maintains ties through visits, calls, e-mail, and Christmas cards. "I hear about potential opportunities within their teams or maybe others that they've heard about. So as people move about the company, I stay in the loop."

She builds rapport with coworkers by paying attention to their vocal inflections on the phone and keeping notes about their personal lives. She knows who has a Siamese cat and whose daughter plays soccer. "Such relationship management requires more effort when you're virtual, but it's worth it." Her boss is pleased with her performance "She volunteers to do extra things and sees them through. She has taken leadership on projects and delivers as promised."[9]

SUGGESTIONS FOR NETWORKING

Many people ask us how to develop better networks. They know they need to develop them, but they don't know how to start. It's a real issue, and so we're always looking for solutions. We talked to a number of people to see if they had some interesting suggestions for networking. In addition, we had experience with some good ideas ourselves. Below are a number of ideas you may want to try to improve your networks—and consequently your visibility and mentoring opportunities as well. Some will work well for you, others may not, but I think they're all worth considering.

1. **Make an event of anything you can think of.** Find an excuse to be face to face with colleagues and/or customers. Important mile-

stones, sales targets, welcoming a big new customer, monthly or bimonthly anniversaries of team and department members, the successful installation of a new computer system—all these things can be fun. Invite colleagues from other departments as well as customers (internal and external) and don't make it a big production. Don't spend much (if any) money. E-mail them invitations for cake and coffee at 3 P.M. or bagels in the morning in your office area, maybe a six-foot "hoagie" sandwich at lunchtime, homemade brownies, or chocolate chip cookies. Believe me, if there's food, they'll come. Give your team a chance to shine and talk about its success—and let others share their successes, too. Your colleagues and customers will love the chance to get together and talk. Remember, you're building relationships.

2. **Participate in new networking formats.** At a recent American Society of Training and Development (ASTD) conference the organizers held a participant networking cocktail party. It was outstanding! As the hundreds of participants arrived, they were given a sheet of paper with eight to ten discussion topics, all color-coordinated to specific tables. Upon entering the room, participants looked for the tables, with signs and color-coordinated balloons, at which participants with similar interests were seated. Categories included International, Technology, Being a Consultant, Recent Trends in Human Resources, and so on. I randomly sat at one of the "International" tables—with all strangers. As I sat down, I realized that all of them were from Germany or Austria. They were speaking German, of course, and most of them seemed to know one another, but they immediately switched to English when I sat down. This could have been a very awkward situation, but they were charming and welcoming. We talked about differences and similarities in our cultures, organizations, and education. We talked about travel and family. What a wonderful experience.

I confess that if the format of the event had been different, I probably would have felt extremely uncomfortable with 500 people. I would have stood at the food table or bar, talked to a few strangers, and left, thinking that it had been a waste of my time. But with this format it was targeted to my interests and very informative—a great use of my limited time at the conference. It could be used for many topics, internally and externally focused, to maximize networking time and effectiveness, especially for people who are quiet and reserved. The arrangement made it easy to network with people with similar interests but different perspectives.

3. **Volunteer outside the office.** A major consulting firm sponsors teams as an opportunity for employees to assist senior citizens and those who are disabled by renovating or updating their homes at no cost. It's a great opportunity to get to know others in your firm at all levels, as well as community members, while volunteering for a good cause. They paint, do minor plumbing or electrical work, do cleanup work and other activities, and have a great time. Imagine fixing a leaky faucet with your division president. Talk about developing good relationships.

   Participants are also highlighted in internal newsletters and thanked publicly for their service, increasing their visibility as well-rounded members of the community. Other organizations participate in community literacy programs, soup kitchens, job shadowing for high school students, partnerships with elementary or middle schools, on-site visits for young people, computer literacy programs, Habitat for Humanity programs, and many other programs. In addition to the outstanding opportunity to help others, participants can expand their networks internally (with all levels of the organization) and externally (education leaders, government officials, and members of the community).

4. **Join a professional organization.** Another leading consulting firm started to examine the viability of a grassroots network for women in consulting. Since a formal association had not yet been founded, this network looked to provide a forum in which women could discuss topics of interest and share insights with other members of their industry. External associations or networks are often an effective way to benchmark and share experiences with others.

Some of our clients provided great suggestions, describing what they do to encourage networking:

We started a monthly cultural diversity day in our regional headquarters. Employees from different countries work with the employee activity committee to present events to raise awareness of various cultures. It might be food in the cafeteria, discussions of holidays, etc.

ᴄᴧᴕ

Our operations division hosts "A Night in Operations." Various groups arrange to serve pizza and give a brief overview of their business to colleagues outside of that business unit. The food usually gets them in.

ᴄᴧᴕ

We don't make all events family events. Sometimes employees have indicated that they would like to have some time to network, get to know colleagues better, etc., without always having everyone's families there. So now we do a mix of types of events, family and employee-only.

GRASSROOTS NETWORKS

Many times a specific network doesn't yet exist to meet your needs. Sometimes you start your own grassroots network. It can be informal or highly structured, internal or external—it depends on your needs and organization. Some people have discovered that many of their colleagues enjoy reading, and so they start a monthly book club at work, meeting at a lunch table and bringing a brown bag lunch. Other groups can be slightly more structured.

A few years ago when Lynn was working for a huge multinational firm, she received an e-mail from a colleague in Sydney, Australia, asking her, "Do you have any more information on the attached e-mail?" That e-mail said: "A couple of us think that Internet marketing is going to be really big, and we figured that other people in the company might be interested in it, too. So we're going to get some people together for a day in Atlanta and invite a few speakers, have an informal lunch, and see what we can learn. It will cost $75 plus airfare—pass the word." Lynn thought, Yeah, this sounds good. She went and realized that sixty of her colleagues from all over the world had had the same idea. In one session she was seated next to a colleague from London who mentioned that her division was considering opening a small office in Latin America. Lynn's division was considering the same thing and suggested that they look into sharing space. "It was the best event I ever attended—informal, lots of dialogue, great networking." It was an opportunity to meet her corporate colleagues in an informal, nonthreatening, high-energy environment. And it started with just a couple of guys sending out an e-mail.

At a presentation for a major consulting firm in London we were discussing starting grassroots networks: how to do it, what benefits there may be, and so forth. As the group was describing their views and suggestions of why and how to start a network, a young manager shared her views on networking, specifically, how she regretted not having started a grassroots network. She had been abroad as an expatriate for her company, and everything was going fine. Like many young professionals she was busy at work. She shared this story with us:

"When I was an expat, I knew that there were obviously a lot of other people in the same situation, away from home, new customs,

getting to know your way around the new city—and the company itself. Looking back on it now, I would have taken the initiative to start a grassroots network of like-minded people, both locals and expats, to get together, have fun, and share ideas and experiences. I wish that I had done it now, because I would have met a lot more people than just the people I mostly worked with and probably had a much better international experience." Coincidentally, at this workshop in London (now back home for her), she met another woman who had been working in the same office as an expatriate at the same time she was there. They had never met at that time.

Two leaders talked about how they created networking opportunities:

When I was the U.S. liaison officer between the American and German armies in Germany, I revived an old custom and had new officers and their spouses call on us each quarter. This gave them an opportunity to see me and for me to see them (I had about 125 officers in all, and the turnover was rapid). Since we lived in a former World War II general's quarters and had a grand piano and a "music room," we had quarterly "music nights" at which those who were musically inclined could perform. This proved quite popular and provided another informal opportunity for contact.

∽

What crossed over well from my military career? The camaraderie, getting to know each other outside of work. Social events as well. In the military we would have social events in which everyone, including families and spouses, would get together for a once-a-month Italian night or something. It was good to build a social support network, relationships, camaraderie—the support network carried over through the good times and, more importantly, in the tough times.

Here are some questions you may want to consider in creating a grassroots network:

- ♦ Will you be starting your own special interest group or becoming more involved with an existing one?
- ♦ Are there groups or chapters at your organization?
- ♦ Whom do you need to contact?
- ♦ What permission may you need to start your own network?
- ♦ Who needs to be included in the loop if you start your own?

- Who will you identify at your organization who has already begun a new special interest group? How did they do it? What was their experience with the process?

- Can it be on-site or off-site?

- What costs may be incurred?

- How are you going to start? What will the design look like?

- How often will you have events or gatherings?

- Are you going to have—or need—a formalized plan? If so, who is going to spearhead it?

- Are you going to hold regularly scheduled meetings (monthly, semi-annual, annual)?

- Are you going to have officers?

- What's the next step after today?

SUMMARY
Success Secret #5: Build Effective Networks

- Build your communities of practice: internal or external groups with similar interests or goals.

- Develop your network (and possibly find potential mentors) both at work and outside work, with women and with men.

- Investigate "nontraditional" networking sources such as volunteer opportunities, social activities, and sports. Networking isn't always planned. Informal networks often yield the best relationships.

- Start a small grassroots networking group of your own. Determine how it will look and what you want from it.

- Examine and benchmark other groups that have developed networking opportunities. Talk to the members or founders. How did they start? What is their premise? How successful are they? How structured is it? Do they have a formalized organization, or it is more informal? What would work best for your group?

For a list of research participants, please see page xvii.

Gain Global Experience and Insights

༄

Companies led by a chief executive with more international experience perform better in their return on investment, return on assets, and market-to-book ratios.[1]

We have emphasized the importance of performance and results a lot throughout the book, but how can one quantify the impact of gaining international career experience? According to a recent survey, chief executive officers (CEOs) from major corporations throughout North America, Europe, Latin America, and the Asia/Pacific region considered the building of multicultural business teams their third highest priority.[2] Multicultural experience was shown to be correlated directly with good financial performance. In general, however, North American executives placed less emphasis on this experience, and it was concluded that they were missing out on opportunities for developing effective leaders in an increasingly global business environment. A number of our participants shared their advice and experiences:

If I had to give several pieces of advice to young leaders, developing global awareness would be one of them.

༄

Globalization does not mean losing the individual identity of the other countries. It is important to be respectful of local customs and attitudes and to implement strategies locally.

༄

The world really is a small place. In Asia I found a need to listen to others' approaches to solving problems—yours is not the only way. And in business there are a lot of type A personalities who don't always listen.

⌖

Be open and awed by others, including their differences. True team-work requires a diverse set of skills and perspectives. Don't just talk the talk of diversity; embrace it in all its forms. The strength of the team comes from the diverse experiences of the team members.

⌖

I finally realized that it was because I was different that I brought a new and often different perspective to viewing the issue. But at the same time, I felt that perspective was not "right." I should have realized that my different way of analyzing the problem, seeing a different solution and often a different path to achieve the goal, was a value I added.

PriceWaterhouse Coopers' annual survey of 800 to 900 CEOs in major industrialized regions of the world asked about the importance of international experience. Many of the CEOs responded that they were sensitive to global issues, but very few had had international experience.

To put it in more concrete terms, researchers at Indiana University's Kelley School of Business examined the impact of international experience on a manager's likelihood of promotion to the top and on the firm's financial performance (international experience was defined as the number of international assignments and the number of years in those assignments).[3] Based on the results assembled from a number of Fortune 500 corporations, specific themes emerged, including networking internationally, communication and cultural awareness, global teams, international image and competencies, developing a multicultural and multidisciplinary matrix, technology, and strategic issues in leadership development. Not coincidentally, those issues reflect many of our participants' views. Here are some thoughts on these various issues.

INTERNATIONAL ASPECTS OF NETWORKING

Many people—and Americans are probably the most guilty of this—feel that there is one most effective way to network: Go to events, pass out business cards, and meet people like gangbusters. "Of course they'll give us business or let us in on a great new job opening!" Don't laugh, but this still happens—a lot. At the other extreme, many of us are hesitant to ask any kind of "favor" in our network: We feel that we shouldn't put someone out. Is there any happy medium? It depends on your frame of reference. Not everyone in the world approaches networking in that same way.

Lynn and I wrote about this in our last book, *Seven Secrets of Successful Women,* but I think it should be underscored for those of you who have not read it. Several years ago the European Women's Management Development Network did research on international network styles and outcomes. They interviewed women from three countries: the United States, the United Kingdom, and Spain. The findings were interesting. American women were called "Instrumentalists." They liked to get down to business, be visible, and get the job done. British women were called "Developers." They enjoyed learning and developing skills in their networking, and they did more external networking than internal. Finally, the Spanish women were called "Socialites." They didn't specifically want to do business networking—they preferred getting together in a café where they could drink coffee and talk to their friends for hours. (When I bring up this example in seminars, many Latin women come up to me at the break and say, laughing, "You're right. That's exactly what I like to do.")

Ironically, when asked about the business outcomes from their networking efforts, it was the Socialites who had done the most business as a result of their networks. We have seen it in action. A colleague of Lynn's named Flavia is from Argentina. Lynn said, "I've never seen anything like it. We would be walking through an airport in some obscure city, for example, and we would hear someone call out from the crowd, 'Flavia, hi!' It was the most amazing thing. No matter where we went on business, there was someone who knew her, knew her family, went to school with her sister, and, of course, as a result of her networks, she brought in tons of business in Latin America. I can attest to her networking skills."

The number-one message here? Develop relationships—long lasting, two-sided, mutually beneficial relationships. When people care about you and like you, they want to help you—and you want to help them.

We all know about the value of building relationships in improving one's business prospects, but is that relationship always going to look the same in Japan, in Italy, in Brazil, in Australia? How do you navigate the subtleties? Once again, tap into your own networks. Ask around—find out who's worked or at least spent some time in the region you'll be dealing with. Do your homework ahead of time. There are a lot of good books on the subject that will get you started. Go online and do some research.

One big piece of advice: Go prepared, armed with up-to-the-minute information. This is a situation where you probably won't get any feedback once you're in that setting. In many cultures, particularly in Asia, your counterparts probably will be too polite to let you know when you're committing a faux pas.

INTERNATIONAL COMMUNICATION AND CULTURAL AWARENESS IN BUSINESS

An emphasis on developing an effective, highly aware communication style came up time and again among our participants as an important factor in career success. This takes on added significance in today's increasingly global business environment. This doesn't apply only if you're working for a huge multinational firm. Smaller local companies also need to address the needs of workforces that are multinational, multiracial, and multiethnic. With the onslaught of technology in all businesses, you never know where your clients might be coming from. I recently saw an interesting television program in which a small modular-home-building company in the middle of Pennsylvania had forged a partnership with builders in Japan. Since in that country limited land availability and high building costs limit home ownership, the Japanese builders go to Pennsylvania to learn about the process—and place their home-building orders there. The company's owner said, "I never thought that I would be working with primarily Japanese home builders and that I would have to develop a complex process of accommodating diverse taste in styling, adhering to foreign building codes, and shipping prefab houses halfway around the world."

Here are some other insights from senior executives on the importance of having a global perspective.

Dr. Koichi Nishimura, CEO of Solectron, believes that "ordinary people do extraordinary things, given the right environment. . . . My grandmother taught me about Japanese values, all of which I have installed in the Solectron culture. Although the values may seem very Asian at first, they are quite universal. She taught me the meaning of virtue and the accumulation of it. . . . We talk about the same thing with our associates."[4]

∽

Problems are generally not logical or mathematical. Crossing ideas from different horizons and diverse populations brings about a response of "Aha! This is interesting!" It might not always result in the absolutely best possible solution, but it brings up better solutions than you would have found on your own. We're not like computers that always give the same response when you program in the same information.

∽

Diversity is going to be one of the most important issues in the next decade. Things are changing at 1,000 miles per hour. It's not just gender and race. I'm on the board of a fiber optics company in Silicon Valley. There's not a company out there that doesn't have a broadly diverse employee base. You have to understand the subtleties. For example, there are differences in "Chinese" culture, depending on whether your employee is from Hong Kong or from Malaysia. Attitudes need to change in the twenty-first century.

◌◌◌

The most relevant leadership development exercises involve working in teams of individuals of different expertise, backgrounds, ethnicity, gender, and international perspective. In other words, they must reflect the realities of today's global business environment, the environment in which we all will be called upon to lead.

The greatest advantage of the rich diversity of today's workplace is that it brings the breadth of ideas and perspectives best suited to promote innovation. Innovation happens in the cracks: between one field of specialization and another, between my idea and your idea. The quality of an individual's leadership will be measured by the way he or she welcomes differences of opinion and perspective, how he or she utilizes the diverse backgrounds and experiences of the team members, and how the team focuses all this energy into productive work. One of our alumni, David Pottruck, president and co-CEO of Charles Schwab Corporation, calls this "leading from the middle."

Don't make assumptions about communication and business styles abroad. With all the talk of globalization, there are still many different approaches, which one must understand in business. Lynn and I have traveled, studied, and worked internationally for over twenty years, during which Lynn spent fifteen years conducting business all over the world for huge multinational corporations. Even with a degree in foreign languages and varying degrees of proficiency in seven languages, she still has her assumptions challenged occasionally.

Several examples are highlighted below, demonstrating some of the cultural subtleties to keep in mind while conducting business around the world. Research on various factors to consider in developing business relationships in international markets concurs with our own experience as well as with that of our colleagues. You may want to keep the following ideas in mind.

In most Latin countries, in both Europe and in the Americas, relationship-building is an important aspect of conducting business. The setting often includes food and wine.

In France, business is conducted in a somewhat formal manner, but food and wine are also an important component of the business process.

Conducting business in Germany also involves a formal manner (although this is beginning to relax somewhat) and punctuality is important. Titles are also used more frequently; my father often received correspondence from Germany addressed to "Herr Professor Doctor Brooks."

In Scandinavia and in the Netherlands, communication is often quite direct, and business can generally be conducted in English. Technology and innovation are also important components in Scandinavian business.

In Japan, building relationships and consensus and observing hierarchy are important aspects of successful business development. Doing your homework beforehand is also crucial to the process.

Lynn recalled a conversation following a colleague's first business trip to Japan. "I went there with five prepared contracts in my briefcase. In four out of the five initial client meetings, we never got beyond drinking tea!" Her former boss also shared this advice on doing business in Japan: "It's often difficult to determine who the main decision maker is in a meeting. Read the dynamics of the room. The most senior person often says little, but you can tell a lot by everyone's body language."

In the United States, business relationships are generally informal and more direct than in other countries. Negotiations get down to business quickly, and results are the measure of a successful meeting.

KEY ISSUES FOR WORKING GLOBALLY

Here are some of the other differences that you may encounter while communicating globally at work.

Participating in and Leading International Teams

We've seen that one of the keys to a successful career is the ability to work comfortably in a team setting: project management. But there are special issues that arise when that team is global. And now, thanks to technology, there's a new expression in the business lexicon: "virtual global teams." Here's what one person says about this subject:

> *When global teams fail, it is often due to a lack of trust among team members. Also high on the list of culpable factors are the hindrances to communication caused by geographical, cultural, and language differences.*[5]

Lynn, like many other employees working for multinational firms, had to frequently juggle time zones in order to contact colleagues and clients.

That meant getting on the phone to Tokyo at midnight or at 5:30 A.M. to catch colleagues in Europe. We asked some of our clients to share some of the challenges they face working with their colleagues around the world.

> *Our operations unit works on 24/7 schedule worldwide, with offices in the United States, Europe, and Asia. Key staffers from each region have collaborated to arrange regular virtual meetings to accommodate everyone's schedules and time zones. Management at the various offices has helped out in the process by allowing employees to adjust their work hours to accommodate the time zone differences for these meetings rather than requiring the participants to do it "after hours" from home or the office.*

∽

> *The most effective virtual team leaders act in a mentoring role, exhibiting a high degree of understanding and empathy towards other team members. They found effective leaders extremely good at providing regular, detailed, and prompt communication with their virtual teams and articulating role relationships (responsibilities) among the virtual team members.[6]*

International Image and Competencies

Our participants talked a lot about creating a career "tool box" for international jobs. One executive from outside the United States offered his perspective on important skills for international business.

> *Fluency in English is important to success in a multinational business environment. Whenever possible, try to gain one or two years of experience outside your native country. This will help you master English as well as develop an openness to others' cultures—you'll be able to think outside the box.*

A study published by the Association of Executive Search Consultants Europe pinpointed a shortage of top management with the necessary international and cross-cultural skills as the major obstacle to European integration. The successors of today's CEOs will need to outperform their predecessors in areas such as adaptability to new situations, international strategic awareness, ability to motivate cross-country teams, sensitivity to different cultures, and international experience. Maury Peiperl of the London Business School concludes: "Clearly, many companies in Europe still need to face the impending shortage of top management talent head on. . . .

The new European CEO—adaptable, internationally experienced, fluent in a variety of cultures—must lead these companies not only throughout Europe, but in the wider global marketplace."[7]

International Relocation

A number of our participants pointed out the difference between traveling internationally for business and actually spending a period of time working in a different environment. (The latter was seen as a major career enhancer.) While international relocation is not for everyone, the perception is that women in general aren't interested in international assignments. If it's something that you might want to pursue, make sure you let that be known. Once again, don't assume that people can read your mind.

Some of the most valuable lessons I learned came from growing up and living in a number of different countries and cultures. The beginning of my international career experience coincided with a time when organizations were becoming more international and seeking individuals with global perspectives. I was more comfortable living in different cultures than many of my colleagues were. I genuinely liked the environments in which I lived. I enjoyed spending time with the locals. I feel I led by gaining the respect of people who worked in the more far-flung corporate "outposts."

ско

What would I have done differently? I have traveled extensively in my career and have developed, I believe, a cultural sensitivity. I lived in a country for a project, for example, and spent time on every continent, but I wish I had had more focused experience of living and working in a country for one or two years—or more.

Creating a Multicultural/Multidisciplinary Matrix of Skills

In keeping with the theme of gaining broad-based experience, many of our participants emphasized the value of combining a diverse background in both content area and culture—creating a matrix. Among their insights were the following:

What's usually missing in young leaders is a "multidimensional cross development." By that I mean multicultural development and business development (sales, operations, etc.). Different countries have different ways of doing business. Emotional intelligence develops differently in various cultures. You develop different ways of looking at things.

⚬∿⚬

I would urge people to live abroad for a period of time. Also, I would recommend that people have as many work experiences as possible. I didn't always have a finance position. As the president of my company's Asia division, I had to deal with sales, distribution, operations . . . not necessarily only the finance end of things. It was a wide range. But I found later that it was very helpful when talking to my colleagues about all of their issues, situations, problems or challenges. I could discuss them in depth; I could say, "I've done your job."

⚬∿⚬

Many women running technology firms in Canada came from non-technology backgrounds. Zita Cobb, EVP, Strategy & Business Development at JDS Uniphase, parlayed her background in finance (joining as CFO) into a key role in the creation of the world's biggest fiber-optic equipment company.[8]

International Aspects of Technology

Some view technology as the great equalizer in career opportunity. Others see it as the new "glass ceiling" for women. In either case, a comfort level with today's technology is one of the competencies that's mandatory for career success. Several executives shared their opinions in research studies:

There's nothing preventing women from making lucrative, rewarding careers in technology companies—gender is not an issue. Capability, enthusiasm, and energy are.[9]

⚬∿⚬

Latin America's top executives are the only regional group of CEOs predicting that the Internet will ultimately level the global playing field. They firmly believe that e-business will throw the doors wide open for emerging market companies to cross borders that, until recently, were barriers to everyone but the multinational giants.[10]

⚬∿⚬

Technology companies aren't luring women because of a sense of obligation. It's because they recognize that solving problems and responding to customers requires a wide range of thinking.[11]

IMPORTANT CHARACTERISTICS IN INTERNATIONAL LEADERS

Many research projects that study strategic issues start with the question, What keeps CEOs awake at night? It's interesting how universal many of the issues and concerns are. Understanding and anticipating these concerns is crucial to succeeding in a global business environment. One recurring theme is attracting and retaining outstanding talent. According to the *Hewitt Asia Quarterly*, the "Biggest People Issues for CEOs and Senior Executives" in the 2001 regional survey include the following.[12]

Hong Kong

♦ Attracting and retaining talent

♦ Growing and developing talent

♦ Aligning employees with business objectives and increasing engagement

Japan

♦ Developing talent required by the business

♦ Developing creative and innovative ways of thinking

♦ Finding and continuously developing appropriate skills

Korea

♦ Developing skills required by the business

♦ Communicating the organization's vision and strategies

♦ Attracting and retaining talent

Singapore

♦ Developing talent

♦ Finding appropriately skilled staff in high-tech and engineering fields

♦ Attracting and retaining talent

Taiwan

♦ Attracting and retaining talent
♦ Developing employees for management positions
♦ Growing and developing talent
♦ Improving the people management skills of managers

Thailand

♦ Developing talent
♦ Retaining people with high potential
♦ Nurturing an innovative culture

These issues are echoed in the CEO Challenge Report 2001 published by Accenture and the Conference Board. Over 500 CEOs were asked to rank the top challenges in the coming year in each of the areas of marketing, management, and technology. Attracting and retaining new leaders, particularly in the area of technology, are seen as especially important in many organizations worldwide.[13]

Topic	North America	Europe	Asia	Worldwide
Marketing challenge: shortage of key skills among employees	Rank: 1	Rank: 3	Rank: 8	Rank: 5
Management challenge: competing for talent	Rank: 2	Rank: 1	Rank: 9	Rank: 3
Technology challenge: impact of the Internet	Rank: 4	Rank: 1	Rank: 2	Rank: 2

SUMMARY
Success Secret #6: Gain Global Experience and Insights

♦ Be open to—and prepared for—leading diverse teams as well as virtual teams.

♦ Be aware of cultural differences when networking.

♦ Understand differences in communication across cultures.

♦ Take advantage of opportunities to live and work in other countries and cultures.

♦ Use technology to facilitate team building, networks, communication, and scheduling challenges for global teams.

For a list of research participants, please see page xvii.

Take Charge of Your Own Career

⚛

I think that in most organizations distinctions between men and women in regard to what one needs to do to be successful have been reduced dramatically. Therefore, I believe that women (and men) need to do similar things to be successful— show commitment to a successful career, be engaged in charting the path of their careers, and identify and work closely with those who can help them develop.

Some statistics say that we can plan on changing careers—not jobs—at least five times in our lives. You can make a choice between allowing the current to take you on any career path and actually setting a conscious career goal. Which have you done?

DEFINING YOUR PERSONAL CAREER STRATEGY

One important goal of this book was to find out how many people make career decisions. Therefore, in addition to interviews with senior executives and leaders, one of our other approaches was to ask a number of people, primarily early-career and midlevel managers, to complete questionnaires in which they talked about their work lives and career strategies.

Interestingly, one observation made by both men and women in our questionnaires was that men tend to set specific career goals more often than women do. Is this true? I don't know. Of course there are many women who chart their careers with clarity, preparation, and direction, but I tend to *hear* more men than women talking about specific career goals. They may not necessarily know the specific job or even a field, but I often hear men say things like "I plan to make partner by thirty-two, be a vice president by thirty-five, make my first million by forty, retire by fifty. . . ." Of course, whether they have a plan for achieving this is another story, but they're *thinking* about their goals. (Yes, I know. Probably some of you are saying, "You're wrong. Every woman I know has had a clear career goal." But even some of the senior women we interviewed said that they had had a zigzag career path and were surprised that they ended up where they were.)

One executive shares her experience:

> *Take time to develop and keep in mind your forward goals. Over time, I have tried to always look at least two years ahead. It's not that you can be absolutely certain how things will pan out, but if you don't at least have some thoughts about what the next steps are for you, when opportunities present themselves, you won't be able to respond appropriately or quickly. It also means that you will shape your development efforts to support the way you want to go. I made the mistake of not planning early enough, right up into my early thirties, when I learned a big lesson.*
>
> *I was a member of a very small program team leading a huge organizational change in the company I worked for. We had around 230,000 employees, and the whole company was restructured during the course of a year. It was only after the event that I realized that all the other team members, except for one (male) friend, had taken the opportunity during all the planning and discussion to identify their next career moves and to ensure that those moves happened as part of the program. Three months before the implementation of the whole project it finally dawned on me—and by that time they were all assigned to their senior posts. I felt very naïve and rather stupid. Although it turned out okay in the end, I resolved that I would never again miss out on the reshaping of the organization (which happens again and again). Seek to be active and a participant during times of change, not passive.*

However, whether many of our participants have or have not set specific goals to be a chief executive officer (CEO) or division president early in their careers, there is one common thread among our senior men and women. They know what motivates them; they have a clear understanding of what their skills are and what they need to develop. Here's what some of them had to say:

> *Throughout my career I have gotten as much education as I could. I believe in broadening your capacity to do things. I have tried to take*

everything in life as a new adventure. I graduated from Annapolis and have another degree in engineering, but at age forty-four I decided to get a law degree. I couldn't have anticipated my career success when I was younger. It's good to have some direction, but sometimes you don't want to overplan your life.

༚

Start out with a basic set of tools, whether they be personality, analytical skills, or a winning combination of humor, a broad view of things, and the ability to articulate and communicate your ideas. Then work on things that you're not strong in to become very broad-based and well rounded.

༚

Realize that success requires a lot of hard work and takes a long time—it's not necessarily like the experience of the dot-com start-ups.

༚

My advice? It's basic, but try to find something you really like—it's not always easy. And find a mentor whom you respect and try to emulate him or her.

༚

Pick your company carefully—companies differ greatly. Look at who has corporate universities and how they develop their people—development is not accidental.

༚

Many people tend to pick roles that are safe and comfortable, but these roles often offer less opportunity for advancement. Find out which skills—as well as which departments—are going to facilitate your advancement. For example, in most companies there's usually only one leadership position in human resources or communications but many more options when you have a finance, marketing, or accounting background. Look for line position experience whenever possible.

One senior executive explained that he had had a very nonstandard career: After twenty years as a consultant, he started at the top, with a high-level job at a major corporation. (He laughs about his career advice to others: "I guess that this strategy did work pretty well—start at the top.") But joking aside, this is especially true for many people who would like to follow his lead and work for a large multinational organization as well as for those who are entrepreneurial and wish to start their own company eventually. Don't forget, he had gained twenty years of effective experience that was directly applicable to his new position in a corporate setting. This illustrates the importance of developing transferable skills.

DECIDING WHAT YOU'RE GOOD AT AND WHAT YOU ENJOY

When I talk about defining your career strategy, I'm not saying that you have to set a career goal at twenty-one and stick to it for the next fifty years. But the strategy for choosing jobs and even careers should stay the same. Ask yourself, What am I really good at? What do I love to do? What am I known for? You may not be able to envision the specific job or the technology may not have been developed yet (who could have foreseen e-business fifteen years ago?), but the elements of the work should be easily transferred. Do you like working with people or tasks? Are you comfortable leading others, or do you prefer working alone? Are you a "fixer," a problem solver, a team builder, someone who can create something from nothing, or someone who gets the job done?

If you ask a lot of our participants what they are known for, they usually don't have to think about it for very long—they can tell you right away. They understand the big picture about their career skills, if not always their specific goals. And of course they know that transferability of their skills across firms and even industries is increasingly important.

We asked senior men and women about their career skills, what they're known for, and how they think others see them. Think about it. Can you be as specific about your skills and talents, what you're known for, and where your expertise lies? Here are several of their comments:

I like to start new projects. I've been in three start-ups so far. I really like starting with a blank page and creating something from nothing. This company is now pretty well under way, so I'll probably be looking for a new challenge soon.

ᐤᣔᣚ

I'm known as the "fixer." I'm good at solving existing problems— turning around unprofitable divisions, increasing international market share. I don't really like starting projects from scratch. I thought about taking a new job that had great potential, a start-up, but when I examined my skills and interests, I realized that I probably wouldn't like it—or be as good at it. You have to know your skills—and your limitations—and try to make the best fit for your personality.

ᴄᐧᖾᴏ

I would say that I'm definitely a change agent. In terms of capabilities I am better at analyzing and fixing a situation or business I inherit than at starting something from scratch. In doing so, I tend to be results-driven and bottom-line-focused. I am not a creative, blue sky thinker.

LEARNING THE RULES OF THE GAME: PERFORMANCE . . . PLUS

If you asked me, "What was the *number-one* theme that you heard from senior executives in your research—from both men and women?" I'd have to say that it is the importance of performance, results, and getting the job done. The number of comments like this was overwhelming. When discussing differences between men and women, many of our participants said things like, "No, I really don't see any differences in their skills. In their style, maybe, but as long as they perform, deliver, and do the job well, I don't see any major differences between the men and women who work for me and with me." Marcus Buckingham, coauthor of *First Break All the Rules*, agrees. He states that CEOs love bottom-line performance, numbers, and statistics—they live for them.[1] The message is performance, performance, performance!

"Okay, great," say a lot of women. "If I work really hard, I'll get noticed and rewarded." Wrong! This is only the first piece of the puzzle. Working hard, performance, results, and getting the job done are just the price of admission. It's a given—it gets you *into* the game. Then the unwritten rules of the game come into play.

These unwritten rules are what many successful men and women instinctively know, but many have learned them at an early age, and so they don't think to tell you about them. They have never known life without these skills. But for the rest of us, who don't know the rules of the game in corporate life, these are the subtle lessons we must learn. In addition to outstanding performance, you need visibility, advocates/mentors/sponsors, the right style, and the ability to communicate. Also important is the ability to take risks, lead teams, develop effective networks, convey adeptness in your skills, and demonstrate an understanding of the organizational culture—what is valued and what's not, who shines and who doesn't. Just working hard simply isn't enough. Here's some advice:

Develop a complete understanding of your business and use that understanding to have the confidence to maneuver within the organization. Learn what's valued. Get an early start; find your place as soon as possible.

ᐯᐳ

Earlier in my career I underestimated the power of the intellectual process of learning (graduate school, in my case). I thought I knew a lot, but I didn't. I realized that in order to do what I wanted to do, I needed to go further.

ᐯᐳ

My advice? Get as much practical experience as possible. Take opportunities even when they may not be in your career track. Get transferable skills. I was hired in a bank for a staff position—corporate budget director. The unit boss had just been fired—I was the next guy. I recommend jumping on opportunities. In my case it was in an area that was "screwed up." But I didn't change the people in the unit, I used communication and project management to get them motivated and turn the unit around.

ᐯᐳ

When I left the service after Vietnam in 1974, I had a hard time getting a job. It was difficult for Vietnam vets. Even though I had won the Navy Cross and the Purple Heart, I was rejected by eighty-five companies. But I finally got three interviews. Chase Manhattan happened to be starting a new project in an area in which I had experience, and they wanted someone with midcareer experience, which I had gotten as an officer. It was my transferable skills and performance, I believe, that got me that first position.

WHERE DO I GO FROM HERE?

Are you maximizing your creative talents and abilities, or did you get into your field for the money, the hours, or the prestige rather than because you enjoy it? Give yourself the following assignment: How would I describe my ideal job? But wait. Before you start listing work assignments, titles, and salary requirements, take it back a step. Has your perspective changed over the last several years? Has your life changed, or your interests? I've asked students in undergraduate classes about their perception of the ideal job. It was pretty interesting to hear the results. At the age of eighteen or nineteen, there were some fairly clear ideas of what they wanted—at least in terms of the big picture. Can we say the same? I know that they haven't yet experienced what we have—the harsh realities of the world of work. However, if we want to take charge of our own careers, a fresh perspective often can be interesting. Here are some of the students' ideas:

◆ I want to work in an industry where I can make a difference and where people are valued.

◆ I want to have flexibility in my job.

◆ I don't want to be a slave to work like my parents were. Balance is important in my life.

◆ The money's not that important. A starting salary of about $35,000 to $40,000 is fine.

◆ I want to work in a warm climate like Florida, North Carolina, Arizona, or California.

This sounds a bit simplistic, but when you've decided to take charge of your own career, you sometimes have to start by thinking "simple," not complex. Some very successful people have started to ask the same questions.

For example, there has been a trend among many technology millionaires (who actually did cash out their stock options) to wonder what they wanted to do next in their lives. They had many millions of dollars in the bank. The challenge and thrill of their start-ups had diminished. They felt that much of the meaning had disappeared from their work lives—you can accomplish only so much by age forty. Upon reflection, they decided to take a break from their careers to give back to the community. They did exactly what those eighteen- to nineteen-year-olds did: They asked themselves, What's next? What would be an ideal job?

For one young former senior executive, the answer was encouraging literacy, but not just by funding literacy programs. He also actually sat down on the floor and read with the kids. Another woman, a former technology manager, felt strongly that many African-American children were at a disadvantage in regard to technology. Not only did she fund a computer literacy program for inner-city children, she taught some of the courses. A financial executive decided that he was ready to do volunteer work on the boards of several charities. The president of a major telecom company said he would love to be a university professor for his next career move.

We saw this trend in a lot of the senior executives we interviewed—the concept of reexamining priorities, giving back through volunteerism, doing charity work, helping others. Others have gone in another career direction. Several of the people we interviewed for our last book a few years ago have gone on to start their own companies, relying on the strong skills they gained in the corporate world. Some are authors, entrepreneurs, even professors—transferring their skills to a new environment. Some planned to make the move and carefully identified skills they would need. For others the change was more serendipitous—the right opportunity at the right time.

So what's your next step in taking charge of your career? Consider some of the observations in the chapter summary below.

SUMMARY
Success Secret #7: Take Charge of Your Own Career

♦ Take time to develop and keep in mind your forward goals. Try to look at least two years ahead.

♦ Get as much training and education as you can. Broaden your capacity to do things.

♦ Find out which skills—as well as which departments—are going to facilitate your advancement. Do this as early as possible in your career. Look for line position experience whenever possible.

♦ Understand what companies look for—performance, performance, performance—and learn how to deliver it.

♦ Ask your mentor or advocate if you need advice on which skills you should work on. Leaders seek out those with a strong skill set.

♦ Determine what you like and what you're good at. Do you prefer start-up opportunities? Are you a good problem solver? Do you have a wide range of skills that are valued at your organization? Are you good at fixing existing situations?

♦ Give yourself the following assignment: How would I describe my ideal job? Then start evaluating your skills, experiences, and career gaps as they pertain to that job.

♦ Seek out the tough jobs no one else wants and do a good job on them. Deliver what you say you will.

♦ Pick your company carefully—companies differ. Look at who has corporate universities and how they develop their people. Development is not accidental.

- ◆ Develop transferable skills. It's not necessary to excel at a number of skills. Even one area of expertise is adequate. If you only have one good skill, make sure that you develop it fully. Let others know that you have it.
- ◆ Get broad-based experience.
- ◆ Gain experience working on and leading teams; such experience is essential.

For a list of research participants, please see page xvii.

Develop Winning Communication Skills

ॐ

As you become a leader, your communication skills need to grow as you grow into bigger and bigger jobs. Public speaking, for example, became more important for me. In one position I did a presentation a week in front of thousands of people. As a "numbers guy," I had to overcome that apprehension.

One of the most prevalent themes we heard from our leaders was the importance of communication—listening, persuading, negotiating, and sharing information one on one and in teams. Women are always recognized as being better communicators than men—by both men and women. Interestingly, one of the things that struck me as I interviewed these successful women and men is that, although it's a given that leadership and success require the "harder" skills—understanding numbers, doing analysis, developing strategy, problem solving, and so forth—the "softer" skills were cited more frequently as keys to success. These are things such as listening, leading teams, sharing your passion and drive, and communicating your mission and goals. Men routinely admit that this is where women excel.

If women seem to be innately superior in this area, it would be helpful to fine-tune the communication skills in which many women say they need the most work: negotiation, persuasion, and communication style—simply being heard.

BEING HEARD IN GROUPS, TEAMS, AND MEETINGS

In our research a number of men mentioned that women often seem to be less visible in groups than men are. They speak up less in meetings and are often more tentative in their comments or observations. Interestingly, many of the women we interviewed agreed. With this issue in mind—specifically, being heard in groups, teams, and meetings—we asked women if they have experienced this situation: You're in a meeting or group and bring up an interesting or insightful point or suggestion. Nothing. Then, five minutes later, someone else—it's often a guy—says exactly the same thing, and everyone says, "Wow, that's a great idea; let's run with it." What do you do? Many of us have been in that situation, and we often think to ourselves, Wait a minute, I just said that. Am I invisible? Well, we have asked men and women in our presentations, "How would you handle this type of situation? How would you keep this situation from happening again? What advice or suggestions would you give to others?"

Even if you have never experienced this situation, these are good tips for both men and women for increasing one's visibility in groups, teams, and meetings. Here are some of their suggestions. Maybe one will work for you.

1. Try to get the agenda for every meeting in advance so that you can prepare. Be far more prepared than you need to be. Know what will be discussed in the meeting or discussion, bring additional background information, and be overprepared.

2. Try to get your issues—that is, what you want to discuss—on the agenda in advance, if possible, so that everyone knows that the ideas came from you.

3. Hold back some of the information you want to share; then you can add more information a few minutes later. That way, if someone tries to claim your idea as his or her own, you can say, "Oh, I'm glad you agree with my point, and here's something else that we may want to consider as well."

4. Ask one of your trusted colleagues beforehand to reinforce some of your statements casually during the meeting: "I'd like to go back to a point that Mary made a few minutes ago." Or immediately after you say something, that person can add, "I think that's a great idea." If you have a good rapport with the other person, he or she is usually happy to do it—and you should always return the favor. This is especially helpful if you know that a particular person is bound to try to "steal your thunder" in the group. But it's probably a good thing to do in any group when you want to increase your visibility, especially if your colleague is well respected and can give you greater credibility.

5. Ask a trusted colleague if your communication style is the problem. Can other members not hear you? Are you not speaking loudly or

confidently enough? Do you use too many qualifiers? Do you not use the right jargon or "lingo"? Once you find out what the problem may be, do something positive about it. Listen to how others communicate or even take public speaking lessons.

6. A sense of humor works well in some situations. If it's appropriate, when someone repeats your idea or suggestion, say something like, "Wow, John, I'm flattered that you liked my idea so much that you just *had* to repeat it!" or "Is there an echo in the room?" or "Hello, am I having déjà vu all over again?"

7. Bring overheads, slides, or visual aids whenever possible to remind people who made the point in the meeting.

8. It's helpful to do a follow-up memo or e-mail to the group to sum up what you said at the meeting and perhaps add more details or information. Then there's less question about who originally made the point.

9. When appropriate, volunteer to take the minutes in a meeting to make sure you get the credit in writing for your comments.

Here is one senior woman's explanation of what she did:

My organization was starting a new initiative. Although I was a content expert in the area, I was a lower-level manager at the time and wasn't included in key discussions. I just wasn't visible enough, and no one really knew that I was an expert on the topic. I asked my boss if I could sit in on one of the meetings to see what was being discussed. However, before I attended, I made copies of pertinent articles, research, statistics, and other information that I thought would be of interest and helpful to all of the attendees.

During the meeting the team leader, a senior manager, said, "We probably need more information on this topic." Passing out my information, I said, "Well, I have the information you need right here." This happened three times during the meeting, and each time I passed out information that could answer their questions. By the third time I realized that the key people were starting to ask me questions, and then they included me in a subcommittee to explore additional issues. They hadn't seen me as a viable resource until that meeting—until I could prove my value to their goals.

Another situation that frequently comes up is waiting one's turn to make the perfect point—only it never comes. Then someone else says what you were thinking, and everyone says, "Wow, what a great idea!" And you think, Wait a minute. That was my point, and now someone else looks like a star instead of me. By the way, this is extremely common among both women and men. Speaking up in public can be nerve-wracking. Here are some points from senior managers that may help you shine in groups or meetings in the future:

1. **If you have something worth saying, just jump in and say it.** Don't wait for the right time, for a pause, or for others to take their turn. That time usually never comes. Practice in a low-stress environment, preferably with colleagues with whom you have a good rapport, to get comfortable with hearing your own voice speaking out. Be aware that sometimes you'll do well and other times you may feel less stellar. That's part of the practice—learning your best style.

2. **Work to improve your public speaking and communication skills.** Realize that if you're not especially comfortable speaking up in a group, it's going to take time and hard work to develop this skill. Don't think that you'll try it once and all of a sudden the discomfort will disappear. It won't. Try Toastmasters, a public speaking class at work, or a local college or adult education center. Practice with friends. Rehearse possible situations in advance.

3. **Be unbelievably well prepared.** People can be tough on you and quiz you; make sure you know what you're talking about. Do research, bring statistics, and make it measurable. Plus, if you know a lot about the topic, it's much easier to sound confident, and you will have more of an opportunity to add value.

4. **Encourage others to share their ideas.** If you know that a team member is knowledgeable about a particular area but is quiet and reluctant to speak up in a group, try to create an environment in which that person can share his or her thoughts or draw out that person's opinion to give him or her the opportunity to contribute in a low-stress, nonthreatening environment. But make sure it's an area that team members really know a lot about. You don't want to put people on the spot. They may not be prepared, and they'll feel even more uncomfortable.

5. **Make sure you have something worthwhile to say.** Before speaking up, be sure you're contributing something that will enhance your visibility and credibility. It can be harmful to try to be visible by speaking out with a point that is redundant or weak just to stand out. It may make you look inattentive or just like a jerk.

6. **Take an opportunity to shine.** Especially if you don't talk a lot at meetings, make the moment count and make a positive impact. Know some interesting statistics or the latest research or be able to comment on a new industry trend. You don't necessarily have to know the topic inside and out, but you can make an interesting or intriguing point.

7. **Before you make a statement or point in a group or meeting, make sure you can back it up.** If you say, "We will be able to increase sales by 20 percent if we do this," you'd better be able to back up that statement. Nothing is worse than making a definitive statement and having a more senior person say, "Okay, how are you going to do that?" and not having thought about the details. I know. It happened to me, and believe me, I felt pretty stupid. But I was prepared the next time.

Several senior women at major corporations have shared their experiences with being heard. You may initially disagree with their approach, but before you dismiss it, think of it in context.

There have been times when I have shared my suggestion or insight with a trusted male colleague and have asked him to present it either as a casual comment or as a specific point in a meeting, such as, "Susan and I were talking earlier, and she brought up an interesting point. . . ." In each of my promotions I have always been the first woman ever in that position, and so my teammates have all been men. Believe me, I have experience in being the new kid on the block. Sometimes they have been unsure about me. You know, they just don't know me—I'm not a member of the club. I have often had to develop my reputation and credibility over a period of time.

But depending on the environment, you sometimes have to choose your battles about visibility. What's the bottom line? Do I get bent out of shape that a man has to help me get my point across once in a while, or do I just realize that in this specific situation his voice will be heard with more credibility than mine? And since I only choose men I trust, I feel confident that they'll give me credit for the idea. I know that my voice will be heard eventually—it always is—but it's good to understand the politics of how to get your idea presented in a variety of settings.

~

My company went through a recent merger. In my company everyone knew me, the quality of my work, and my credentials. But now I'm in a different division with people from the other company. Since it's a new division for me, I don't have the same depth of knowledge or expertise. No one knows anything about me. I recently was asked to be part of a very visible team. I was very flattered to be asked, and I'm the only woman. But I realize that I have to make my mark all over again. I decided to bring a technical expert with me to the meetings to address some of the more specific questions that arise—it's a man.

Do I like having to do this after being with the company for fifteen years? No, I resent it. But I also know that politically this is the only way that I will be heard and respected and gain credibility. That's just the way that this part of the company operates. I know that it's only temporary, maybe for a few months, so I can deal with it.

⌒

I'm in international sales, with a lot of my business in the Middle East and Asia. Sometimes it's hard to be heard as a woman; it's a cultural thing. So I often have to have a male colleague with me for protocol. If they don't hear me in meetings, I don't get the business. It's unfair, but sometimes that's just the way it is. You have to understand the politics. But I get the business, and the bottom line is more important to me than my ego.

DO WOMEN COMMUNICATE DIFFERENTLY THAN MEN DO?

It's essential to reiterate that women are generally known and respected for their communication skills, as we mentioned at the beginning of this chapter: listening, paying attention to different perspectives, being empathetic. However, there are several areas of communication style that women need to be aware of. In Chapter 2, both senior women and men suggested that women need to develop a communication style that works with a wide range of people, both women and men. In addition, they recommended that some women may need to be more succinct, get to the point when speaking. This is excellent feedback that most of us will never hear in this sometimes politically correct world—and so I was glad to get more than the sugar-coated version. I suggest carefully watching and listening to people who have outstanding communication styles. Take lots of notes—and practice! Here are some observations:

Women are quicker to use "feeling" verbs and styles and to rely on their intuition, as well as logical analysis, in different situations. I have learned over the years to listen hard to my intuition and am no longer scared to use feeling words, even around a board table. At times it seemed strange to say something like "That doesn't feel right," but quite often—in fact, nearly always—I've learned that if I dissect the reasons for that "feeling," I will find that there is actually a very good reason for listening to it. What these feelings represent— this is just a personal view, but I think that our subconscious is processing and correlating information and ideas all the time.

What these "feelings" and "intuitions" and "senses" are is our subconscious having spotted something that is a mismatch or a concern, and that's the way it's flagged to us. Women are very attuned to these things, and if you grab hold of those feelings and senses, quite often they will lead you to something that can be represented in a much more logical and analytical way. They are a clue to something that is worth listening to.

On a slightly different note, one colleague was amazed at the differences he discovered between the ways women and men communicate.

A friend of mine, a lawyer, shared a humorous story with me about differences in communication and style between men and women. His background has been consistently in very "male" organizations. Then he moved into a corporate environment where his boss was a woman (whom he very much respected). He told me that he recently had gone into a normal staff meeting and arrived a little early. He was just passing the time, writing some notes to himself as the other team members wandered in. As they each walked in, he glanced up. One female colleague arrived, then another woman, and then another. By the time the meeting started, he realized that for the first time in his life he was the only man in a meeting.

I asked him, "So what was it like?" He said, "Donna, it was really interesting. We were sitting around the table discussing a topic, and one person hadn't said anything yet during the meeting. Then someone said, 'So Mary, what do you think?' They actually *asked* her to contribute. Then, as someone else gave her insight, some of the other women said, 'That's a great idea!' And I was thinking, 'Great idea?' Even if you *think* it's a great idea, you never *tell* anyone that you think it's a great idea." In his defense, he's a good guy and his "outrage" was in jest, but he was clearly struck by the differences when in a primarily "female" environment.

How Good Communication Can Improve Retention of Women

One tip for retaining women, especially as they move up in the organization, is to understand their individual perspectives and not make general assumptions about their career paths.

One executive recounts a story of two senior women who have chosen to go to part-time positions while their children are young. He not only supports them in their decision but also keeps the communication lines open, keeping them in the loop. Instead of assuming that the women will not be interested in coming back to challenging full-time positions until their children are older or until they come to him with a request, he contacts them as jobs come up that he feels they may be interested in. He doesn't assume, as many managers do, that they will categorically say no. Situations change—people change. It's difficult to predict if or when someone may want to pursue a position. For the right position at the right time, a woman or a man may change his or her mind, decide that it's worth giving it his or her best shot, and take the job. Also, if she (or he) says no several times, keep asking. The important thing is to keep open the lines of communication and not make assumptions.

The same may be true for an international posting. One cannot assume that because a woman has a family, she will not consider an international position any more than one can assume that about a man with a family. Women have told us that they get frustrated. They want international assignments but aren't considered because the decision makers assume that a woman wouldn't want to uproot her family. Bottom line? Don't assume.

Likewise, as a woman, keep your boss updated on any changes you may have made in your career plan. Don't just hint about your career goals—be specific. If you change your mind and decide that you would like to be full-time or part-time or take on more responsibility or an international assignment, tell your boss and others. Don't assume that *they* can read *your* mind either—they can't.

LISTENING SKILLS: CRITICAL TO LEADERS

In our research women were overwhelmingly cited (by both men and women) as being outstanding listeners. Conversely, both men and women indicated that men need some serious work on this skill. (Yes, many guys know that they don't listen well. Some just may not do much about it.)

However, we were surprised at the number of our male participants who cited listening to their people as one of the most critical skills leaders can possess. Leaders must be interested in others and what they have to say; they have to be curious and empathetic. Have you ever had a boss who always thought he or she had all the answers? They didn't need to hear from you; they were the source of all knowledge. How did you feel about them? As a leader—and I'm talking leadership at all levels, from leading your first small team to being the CEO—one needs to be a dynamic listener: asking questions, gathering information, talking to customers to see what they have to say, and talking to employees to hear their issues.

Develop your listening skills. Be out with your people; talk to them. As a leader, you're entrusted with your employees' lives and families. It's a significant responsibility.

∽

I walk through the halls and also visit thirty-eight sites every year. I make it a point to know the name of every employee. I talk to them, and they know me. It's a two-way street. I'm very much aware of what's going on in the organization. They're part of the decision-making process, and they know that.

∽

It's important as a good leader to be a highly aware listener. If you understand the issues in front of you, you can put them in context to make the best decisions.

∽

It's important to be to the point, very straightforward in communication, etc. Make sure that everyone is clear on where you are and what you're doing. Also, learn to listen to both your clients and your employees. Understand their world.

∽

The most important characteristic for a leader is the ability to be a good listener. This assumes that you are ready to challenge your own ideas on a given subject. This leads to better understanding in decision making.

∽

Really listen to what's being said. In meetings and conversations, what percentage of your time do you spend listening versus trying to get your point across?

PUBLIC SPEAKING SKILLS: CRITICAL FOR SUCCESS

One of the things we have heard a lot from our participants is the importance of their public image when they communicate. They reflect on the company—they *are* the company to the public. When you hear about major crises at most companies, who does the press conference or the interviews on the networks? Who talks to the shareholders? The top leaders. When Ford was faced with its tire nightmares on Explorers, who did you see? Jacques Nasser. When Chrysler had to be turned around? Lee Iacocca. The Microsoft trial? Bill Gates. And many others during the September 11 tragedy. These are just a few of the well-known crises. Leaders at all levels have to be in the public eye every day, communicating with Wall Street analysts, with shareholders, with their employees and customers. How do they do it?

As you can see in the lead quote for this chapter, it comes as a rude awakening when many leaders find themselves faced with this issue for the first time, especially the ones in finance, accounting, or technology (or so they tell me). One CEO shared his experience:

There is one serious skill investment I made later in my career than I should have: developing and honing my public speaking, presentation, and video skills. Most executives never find the time to improve and believe they are just fine on camera or behind the podium. As we all know, most of them are wrong—painfully wrong.

So how do you learn? First of all, assume that you will need to be more in the public eye as your career advances. Either internally or externally, you will be speaking more in front of people. Does this strike fear into your heart? It does that to many people. (By the way, speaking in front of people is up there with death and spiders as the three top fears.) Well, like almost anything else, you need to practice and get advice and training from professionals. One executive shared his thoughts with me during a conference I presented. A senior vice president for a major technology corporation, he did the kickoff keynote for the day. I've rarely seen anything like it: not as much as an index card in his hand as he spoke to 200 people for almost an hour. And he didn't just talk to them—he engaged them, he was funny, he was articulate, he was prepared, he followed a theme. I talked to him after the break and complimented him on his outstanding presentation. He just laughed and said, "Oh, thanks, but I have to admit that I couldn't sleep most of last night because I was so worried about this. I am very nervous speaking in front of people." I was amazed. Of course, I asked him how he did it. He took presentation and public speaking classes and practiced whenever he could. It obviously worked.

Another executive shared his thoughts:

I don't like to admit it, but I really hate speaking in front of people. I'm in finance; I never thought that I would have to do presentations. But now I have to run regular meetings with the operating committee of the firm, so I really have to work on my communication skills.

As you saw in earlier chapters, many senior women across industries are now finding themselves dealing with these issues. When a group of the most senior women in the country went to the Breakers in Palm Beach for a networking weekend, what was one of the topics? Speaking to the media, at analysts' meetings on Wall Street, to the shareholders. It's a new skill that must be learned and practiced. When high-potential women in politics attended the National Association of Legislative Women conference, what was a major focus of the week? Public speaking. Ask the senior people in your organization and they will agree. It is absolutely critical to develop these public speaking skills.

And don't forget, those of you who are not yet being interviewed on international television still need to work on your presentation skills. Develop expertise not only in the actual communication of your points but also in the technology required. It is now frequently Power Point, although in the near future it will have moved on. Whatever the new medium, learn it and become proficient at it. Talk to your technology department or to a friend who can help you. Remember, we're talking about your image here. You can't be using black-and-white overhead sheets without graphics.

NEGOTIATION STYLE

Negotiation is another thing that comes up a lot as an issue for women; a lot of women in our programs ask about it. By the way, many men hate to negotiate too. Maybe it's more of a personality thing than a gender issue. But in any event, more women talk about what they need to learn about negotiating.

There are many outstanding female negotiators, but it takes practice. I'm usually not one to blow my own horn, but I have learned the hard way to negotiate pretty darn well. My first lesson? Years ago when my brand-new car had many major mechanical issues, I was forced to call the president of the company. Nice guy, but I was a psycho on the phone, thinking, like many women, that I had to "do it like a man." I demanded, ranted, yelled (*very* unlike me; ask anyone). When, after four months of phone calls, I finally got a new car, I called the president of the company to apologize for my behavior. He said, "Oh, you were delightful. You should see some of the people I have to deal with!" Delightful? I guess it's all relative. However, I did learn *not* to do it like a man. Even though it worked, it was not an approach that was comfortable for me. I had to find my own style.

If you find that you will need to negotiate a lot in your job, find yourself a mentor. Go with that person when he or she negotiates and watch carefully. See how that person does it in various settings because each one is different. See what works and what doesn't. And start with small things. Believe me, you negotiate every day of your life. Practice—and get feedback. Actually doing it is the best preparation.

Although aspects of the following strategies can work in high-level negotiations, I'm referring more to the day-to-day negotiations we all engage in: the demanding coworker who thinks you're wrong and she's right on every issue, the impasse on a committee decision, salary negotiations, changing departmental or organizational policies, the finance department that wants to cut your budget, even the guy at the car repair shop or the mortgage department. There are many situations in which you must negotiate. That's the best way to practice. Believe it or not, even if you are someone who tries to avoid conflict at all costs, practicing these interactions can be kind of fun.

Some of my male friends and colleagues slyly gave me their observations on how a lot of men negotiate and how to handle it. According to them, men posture, yell, and sound scary while negotiating, but it's usually all an act. Most of the time they don't take it personally, and neither should women. Here are some tried and true strategies for negotiating from a variety of sources. Of course, no two negotiations are ever the same—it always depends on the situation—but some of these strategies may work for you:

- Be strong but don't yell or lose control. It's okay to raise your voice a little but avoid being a banshee.

- Stand your ground.

- Look them right in the eye when you're talking, and don't be the first to blink. (I actually had to do this with a six-foot-five-inch contractor once. I didn't shrink away, and he ended up looking at his shoes instead of at me.)

- Get comfortable with the silence. If the other person doesn't respond to your question or point right away, don't try to fill in the gap with justifications or banter. Just wait for an answer. This is hard but very effective.

- Don't smile very much.

- Know what you want and what you can live without. Ask for more than what you want. That way you can concede things you don't care about.

- Be prepared. Come to the table with clear information, data, and statistics where appropriate.

- Don't let yourself be interrupted constantly. I have found that it helps to say clearly and strongly, "Wait, let me finish . . ." They usually do—even if you have to say it a few times. They eventually get the idea.

- If someone is being patronizing or not taking you seriously, let that person know how you expect to be treated. Be specific. ("I find that you are being very condescending. I expect you to look me in the eye, not interrupt me, and pay careful attention to everything I'm saying. I'm being very professional and expect the same from you.") The worst-case scenario is that when you walk away, he or she will think that you're a "witch." But who cares? You generally get your point across, and they won't do it again.

♦ Be fair—don't expect to win everything and the other person to lose. Be gracious and let the other person feel that he or she came out a winner too.

♦ Understand that the other person may have a style very different from yours. That's okay. In a group there may be shouting, threats, and posturing, but don't let yourself be drawn into that if it doesn't suit your style. Sometimes in a shouting match it's the one with the calm, cool, strong voice who is heard amid the hysteria.

♦ At the end be able to walk away and shake hands with no hard feelings. It's usually not personal. This is a great one to master because you never know when you'll need this person on your side in the future. I've seen men do this many, many times.

One senior woman adds her perspective:

In negotiations men seem to be more oriented toward power, fast decisions in a black or white mode. Women are more skilled at relationships. They see shades of gray and explore issues from different angles. Men come to the negotiation table in full battle armor. I don't do that. I believe that it goes against a woman's nature to be aggressive, rude, or abrupt. I never know how to react to these women, and neither do men.[1]

MORE EFFECTIVE COMMUNICATION: ASK THEM HOW THEY WANT THE INFORMATION

Do you ever wonder why people misinterpret so much of what you say? You wonder how they ever got that idea from what you said. They get confused, annoyed, upset, hostile, defensive—and you're wondering, What the heck is their problem? I was so clear.

It is important to realize that not everyone hears exactly what you're saying. You think you're being clear and direct, but people receive and process information in different ways. There can be a lot of room for interpretation. We were doing a program for a group of young, high-potential employees, mostly with engineering and computer science backgrounds, at a pharmaceutical company. We were talking about preferred communication styles. We asked if they liked using e-mail, voice mail, or face-to-face interaction. During the discussion one young guy said strongly and definitively, "I always use e-mail because I can be absolutely sure that what I say will not be misinterpreted. My meaning is always perfectly clear."

Immediately, two young women just about jumped out of their seats. "Are you kidding?" one asked. "I spend half my time trying to figure out what people mean—or what they want—in their e-mails. I have to write an e-mail back to clarify. Then, when they're copied to a lot of other people, everyone has his or her own issue or question. Sometimes I even have to get together face to face to straighten the situation out."

As you can see, it doesn't necessarily matter what method *you* prefer; you can't please everyone. It's always going to be an issue when you're communicating with a larger group, but if it's one on one or in a small group, just ask the persons what they would like. "What's the best way for you to respond to my issue, question, or comment (i.e., how can I get the quickest answer from you so that I can get on with my task?)? Would you rather respond to an e-mail, leave a voice mail, or meet face to face?" Just ask them. That way you'll spend a lot less time trying to get results—believe me.

> *Understand your audience: What moves people in this particular audience? What do they listen to? What language makes sense to them? For one person, it's going to be dollars; for another, it's going to be the values. You match that language with the way you deliver information—whether you're making a presentation, sending a memo, or cornering someone in the hallway to test out an idea. Figure out the message that moves people, put it into the language they speak, and deliver it in a way that works for them.[2]*

COMMUNICATING IN A CRISIS

As I mentioned earlier, I am writing much of this book in the wake of the September 11 tragedy, which has allowed me to talk to leaders about the issue of leading in a crisis. As several of the leaders have said, "It's easy to lead in the good times, in a good economy. But the test of great leadership is in a crisis."

Nowhere is that more evident than in communicating with your people. Here are several examples that illustrate this sentiment.

> *Any time you're in a crisis the communications level has to be stepped up. In our case it was principally by e-mail. You want to let*

your people know specifically what is going on. There were messages from the CEO, and I sent many messages to my team. People believe that you care more when you communicate the situation to them; they really appreciate it. You also need to communicate about four or five times more than you normally do. Your visibility is key to confidence. This was an extreme case, certainly, but you can apply the same leadership principles to any crisis.

⚭

It is important for all leaders to show a genuine interest in the health, welfare, and well-being of their staff. You can't fake it. Inherent to changing an organization is the possibility of reorganizations and layoffs. Be up-front and honest as much as possible. I believe that "employees can take bad news." The problem comes when the employees see the bureaucracy at work, with all the discussions going on behind closed doors but nothing being disclosed. In a reorganization there is a vacuum of information. It fills with either fact or rumor. Communicating as much as possible (without, of course, revealing sensitive information) takes away a lot of the anxiety.

⚭

Pfizer CEO Henry A. McKinnell offers this advice: "Consultation and communication are essential to leadership in times of crisis. Studies reveal that amidst high levels of environmental uncertainty, powerful and decisive chief executives and top management teams produce better performance, and critical to their success is consultation among members of the top team and open flow of information both up and down the chain of command. People need to know what's happening . . . and leadership must be visible."[3]

COMMUNICATION AND IMAGE: TIPS FOR SUCCESS

♦ Develop presentation and public speaking skills.

♦ Improve one-on-one communication; let people know who you are.

♦ Ask for and receive feedback.

♦ Learn the differences in communication styles.

♦ Adapt communication to the environment.

♦ Learn how to be heard in groups, teams, and meetings.

♦ Develop your personal style in negotiation skills and strategies.

- Use various means of communication to address colleagues' personal preferences: memos, face-to-face talks, brainstorming sessions, e-mail, voice mail. Know what works best with whom.
- Be specific about your goals and interests.
- Be brief and to the point in reports, memos, and meetings.
- Don't assume that people know what you want or what you are thinking. They don't! They can't read your mind.

SUMMARY

Success Secret #8: Develop Winning Communication Skills

- Be specific about your goals and expectations. Don't assume that others know what you're thinking. They can't read your mind.
- Don't take things personally. Most women have not been socialized in the same way as men: sports teams, the military, and so on. Many men can scream at each other one minute and go out for a beer the next. Business is business, not personal.
- Be aware that *gender roles* rather than actual gender may largely influence communication styles. Some women are nurturing; others are more masculine in their characteristics. The same is true of men. It is important not to make generalizations.
- Take the time to develop a personal communication style that works for you. Ask your mentor or advocate for advice on situational strategies.
- Develop personal strategies for being heard in a group or meeting. Be overprepared when you're going to a meeting; also know why it's being held and what the major discussion points are.
- Be sure you have something worthwhile to say in a group or meeting. It is critical to be well prepared for any argument or disagreement. Be able to back up your opinion.
- Be succinct in communication. Don't use a lot of qualifiers. Get to the point, be clear, use only as many examples as necessary, and then move on.

- Develop a communication style that works with a wide range of people.
- Develop critical listening skills. It helps you make better decisions.
- Develop and practice a negotiation style that works for you.
- When you need information from others, ask them how they prefer to communicate. This facilitates a quicker, clearer response.
- Develop your public speaking and presentation skills. They are critical as you advance in your career.

For a list of research participants, please see page xvii.

Develop Key Leadership Skills

∽

Leadership is an art, not a science. Some are more naturally prone to good leadership (the born leader), but all can master the basic skills and practice good leadership all their lives. Study the lives and habits of those you identify as "leaders worth following." Develop your own sense and habits of leadership over time, recognizing that the fundamentals remain the same but the way a leader implements them may change as one's responsibilities change and/or increase.[1]

Anyone who has perused the "Leadership" section of the local bookstore or online bookseller probably has been overwhelmed by the number of titles available. Why so much interest in so many different aspects of and perspectives on leadership? If our senior leaders are representative of organizations as a whole, they are desperate to find and develop the new generation of leaders; there's a critical need for leaders. Many of them agreed that there are not enough strong leaders in their pools for the potential positions. One of the things that we wanted to learn from our participants was how they became leaders: What strategies worked? What were their skills and competencies? What could the rest of us learn to help us in our own leadership development strategies? Therefore, the first question we asked our senior leaders, both men and women, was, "What one or two competencies, skills, or characteristics have been especially helpful in your career?" Here are some of the answers we received.

LEADERSHIP DEVELOPMENT: THE TRADITIONAL MODEL

Useful Skills and Strategies

Deliver results all the time, consistently.

❧

I found that there are several core competencies that worked very well for me. I would recommend these four:

- *There is no substitute for hard work.*
- *Always maintain a sense of curiosity.*
- *Continuous learning—you're never "done learning."*
- *Identify good people who fit and then lead them.*

❧

I always let it be known that I wanted the most difficult jobs, the most challenging jobs. My advice? Take on the most difficult jobs and do them well.

❧

I found that one of the keys to leadership involves good problem-solving abilities. Simplify problems by trying to get to the core issue and resolve it.

❧

I've found that a positive attitude has helped me greatly in my career. There's always a solution to a problem. Having this attitude has allowed me to resolve most challenges and move on with my career.

Learning about Leadership

It's important to focus on leadership from day 1 in a new position. Prior to experiencing "the real thing" it's crucial to learn as much as possible about leadership. We hire primarily chemical engineers. They generally like to solve problems alone rather than in teams and present a neat solution. In our organization everyone spends time with the hourly shift workers to gain an understanding of the people who will be working for you—how they think. Some might see this as a waste of their time, but they're just being shortsighted. The importance of leadership is generally not well understood in the business world.

❧

We are always desperate for talented people, a new generation of leaders. We need people with transferable skills. You don't worry about the gender or race. All you care about is whether they can get the job done: competence.

Decision-Making Ability

You need a disciplined, solid, factual, analytical basis for decision making. Do your homework; most strategic blunders occur from lack of preparation. This is what won cases when I was a lawyer—the hard work behind the scenes. You're always counterbalancing judgments. You can't have 100 percent of the facts, but you don't want to jump to conclusions.

✧

Anyone can lead in good times. What defines a true leader is the ability to make and implement the tough decisions.

✧

It's important to develop the ability to gather all the data you can but then make a decision. Go from the quantitative to the decisive.

✧

If you make a decision and then worry about it, you will spend too much time worrying about the next decision you have to make. Just make the decision and then move on. I'm not saying that I never think about the decisions I've made. I may reassess the situation, but I don't worry about it. I find that some middle managers freeze up with the big decisions. You're going to be wrong at times, but you have to make the decision anyway. You need to make fact-based decisions, gather all the facts. There's a place for emotion, but you need all the facts. Demand the facts; work hard on the facts.

THE EVOLUTION OF LEADERSHIP DEVELOPMENT

Many researchers are beginning to see a more specific evolution of leadership development trends. The authors Ruth Williams and Joseph Cothrel[2] believe that after the period of reengineering and downsizing, an entirely new form of leadership is critical to the renewal and growth of organizations. "People skills and business partnering are replacing number-crunching as the most sought-after abilities."

We heard the same thing from our research participants. Many major organizations agree that the business environment is changing with respect to both employees and customers, and it is critical to reflect those changes in leadership selection. Many of our participants spoke about the emergence of "softer skills" in leadership; this contrasts significantly with the military or sports model of the last generation of leadership. This seems to be counter to the image of the focused, single-minded leader of years ago, the terminator who cared about his or her bottom line but not much else.

When I began doing the research, I assumed that most of the highly desirable skills and competencies would be bottom-line-focused—numbers, analysis, logic, measurements, technical skills—which probably was the case in the last generation of leaders. Although they are still critical, I would say that these skills are now a given, a starting point, an expectation of leadership that by necessity must be augmented by a wide range of other competencies and skills, frequently the "softer skills."

The following quote pretty much sums up the dramatic evolution in leadership development: "Work is changing. Organizations are changing. Careers are changing. Gone are the days when *Fortune* magazine would feature its lineup of the 'toughest bosses'—a salute to the top-down, hard-nosed, kick-ass-and-take-names-later CEOs of big corporations."[3]

Here are additional comments made by our participants when asked, "What one or two skills or competencies have been most important in your career?" We did not select only the ones that would prove our point; these are by far the most representative answers in our research.

Using the old adage "Manage things but lead people," it's important to create a good working environment for your staff. Although there is always pressure to provide bottom-line results, try to balance that with a sensitivity to your employees' needs. Thirty years ago as a junior military officer, I received a note from my boss, a one-star general, on his personal stationery, with two handwritten words: "Happy Birthday." Every year I personally address and sign birthday cards to my 500 staff members. My assistant takes care of tracking the birthdays for me, and we change the card's message every year. Some people might think that's a little corny, but I really think the personal touch makes a difference.

I also try to make sure that I know—and use—all of my employees' names. I recall the impression that Secretary of State Colin Powell made on me years ago, when he was chairman of the Joint Chiefs. Although we attended the same large weekly staff meetings, I was clearly a much more junior-ranking officer. Once, when I saw him at a reception, he said, "Hey, Chuck, how's everything going with you?" Being called by my first name really made me feel that I was an important member of the team.

❧

It's important to "spend time in the trenches." I believe that anyone can be a good leader. Not necessarily a great leader, but at least a good leader. But you must care about your people; they will help you achieve your vision.

KEY LEADERSHIP SKILLS

Listening

Interestingly, one of the strengths of leadership cited most frequently by our participants was the importance of listening. Professor John Quelch, dean of the London Business School, reflects: "Do not respect hierarchy. Go anywhere in the organization to find the answers to your questions. Encourage communication across formal lines. Leaders must decide to listen before they decide to lead."[4]

I must confess that I was surprised to see the number of responses that identified listening as one of the top one or two skills. Keep in mind that women frequently are recognized for their communication skills, especially listening. When we ask, "What can female leaders bring to an organization?" this point becomes even more evident—their listening skills.

Here are some of the comments made by, in this case, male senior leaders:

The most important characteristic for a leader is the ability to be a good listener. This assumes that you are ready to challenge your ideas on a given subject. This leads to better understanding in decision making.

❧

It's important as a good leader to be a highly aware listener. If you understand the issues in front of you, you can put them in context to make the best decisions.

❧

Listening to others is one of the most critical leadership skills. But at the end of the day you have to make the ultimate decision yourself. It's hard to tell people that you hear them but are doing it this way anyway. It usually helps if you say that you've heard their viewpoints and give them your reasons why you're doing something else.

❧

Develop your listening skills. Be out there with your people—talk to them.

Good listening skills are crucial key to becoming a successful leader. Listen, but then come to a decision.

Learn to listen to both your clients and your employees. Understand their world. Spend time listening to your people, problem solving, etc.

Listening and being open to new ideas and viewpoints are critical to leaders. There is nothing more effective in leading others than to truly be willing to listen and understand their viewpoints. And there is nothing more important to your own lifelong learning.

Emotional Intelligence

Another skill that was mentioned frequently was emotional intelligence and keeping one's ego in check. Here are some of our participants' thoughts:

The development of emotional intelligence in today's environment is what differentiates leaders. While it's still very important to develop "technical" skills—things like how to increase market share, problem solving, communication skills, and other general competencies— more important is the ability to develop self-awareness and self-management. Be conscious of the impact you have on your organization. Be able to limit your ego.

Really powerful leaders probably agree that decisions aren't based on their egos. The Fortune 10 leaders are grounded as people; they believe in what they're doing. You can't work on being believable.

A leader has to have an attitude, and I don't mean arrogant. It's more a sense of inner confidence, an edge. You need an insatiable drive to win, and you really have to hate to lose! But avoid intellectual and overt arrogance, the ego, the feeling that "I've arrived."

Executive Randy Alsman shared his thoughts on the style of the new Bristol Meyers Squibb CEO, Peter Dolan. "It became obvious right away that here was a person who wasn't threatened when someone else had a better idea. Instead of the typical dog-and-pony show, with everyone presenting overheads, the meetings were truly frank discussions of the issues. Peter did a lot of listening, and when there was new information, he was willing to change his mind. But once we'd established direction, it was full speed ahead."[5]

Passion

The idea of passion and caring for your people and your team is an especially compelling concept. We heard a lot about passion in our interviews. This too was quite a surprise to me.

The greatest distinguisher of leadership is passion and caring— about yourself, your people, your customers, your company. And it must come from the heart; it's not something that's learned. People are sophisticated enough to know if you're sincere—staff, shareholders, media. They know who's real and who's giving you a line of B.S. Be honest and available; lay it on the line. People need to get the sense that you care.

⌒∿⌒

What helped me in my career? A passion for what I am doing. There is probably nothing more important for careerlong success. If you're not passionate about what you are doing, find something else—quickly.

⌒∿⌒

I am always using the phrase "passionate customer satisfaction." This isn't an academic environment. You have to be willing to cross the emotional barrier.

⌒∿⌒

There are different skills that you use at different times in your career, but I have found that a sense of passion and excitement is something that is consistent. It goes back to something my mother used to say: "If you're not having fun, go do something else." That holds true today, and it's infectious to the people who work with you. If you walk around with a spring in your step, excited, others can't help but feel that passion and excitement as well.

⌒∿⌒

I would give the same advice to women as to men. Success comes from doing work you feel passionate about. I don't think you can be a true leader without passion. Without passion, sometimes you may wonder, Why am I doing this? But a true leader is always asking, What can I do to make things better?

Curiosity, Creativity, and Continuous Learning

A number of our participants cited the need to be curious and have an interest in continuous learning; you can't rest on your laurels. In addition to specific skills such as content expertise and technology, you need to develop a broader range of leadership skills. According to the Oxford Forum for Assessment and Development, one of the main reasons leaders stumble is a lack of the specific skills required for particular jobs. "Individuals may be promoted because of particular technical skills, but as they move towards leadership of an organization, they need to develop general strategic skills and the ability to deal with ambiguity and uncertainty. They need to be able to deal with the paradox that for many, what got them into a leadership role will not keep them there—they need to be able to continually identify and learn new relevant skills."[6]

Here are several comments from our participants:

I never really planned my career, planned to be a CEO. When I was really young, right out of college, I was looking for a job. My brother worked for Procter and Gamble, so I got a job there. I was probably the only nonengineer they ever hired in that position. I didn't know anything about engineering. As I moved up, I was still frustrated. I never knew as much as the engineers; I didn't have the skills. But I was determined. I worked on sciences and technology. It took a long time to learn the skills, but eventually I had the engineers working for me. The secret? Continuous learning, an inquisitive nature.

It's important to have creativity and imagination; a curiosity about things helps you be creative. If all problems were easy, just about anyone could solve them, but they're not. You need a questioning mind.

Some execs believe that they've figured it all out. But you have to adapt, be willing to admit what you don't know and tap your resources. There has to be a certain amount of humility. People forget this. Great people believe there's so much more to know; they learn from their mistakes. They are always trying to learn more.

I've always been action-oriented. I get things done. But I think that my creative side has also been an important aspect of my career.

First, make sure you are a person of depth and substance. It is not enough to simply say, "Follow me, I'm a leader." You must lead by example, and this requires expertise. Continue to develop this expertise throughout your career; don't stop after your formal education ends.

Becoming Well Rounded

One of the traits that was somewhat unexpected, regardless of background or industry, was the image of leaders being well rounded, having broad interests, with an emphasis on continuous learning. Many people have the image of senior leaders being quite narrowly focused on running the business: making tactical and strategic decisions, dealing with stockholders and the board of directors, doing company balance sheets, following market trends, analyzing competitive analysis, seeking new business developments and innovations. I was more than a little surprised when I saw a noticeable emphasis among these leaders on the importance of culture, the arts, literature, language, philosophy, theology, and other interests in their lives.

John Thornton, president and co-COO of Goldman Sachs, reflects, "When hiring people throughout my career, I have drawn on the advice of Siegmund Warburg, one of the giants of our industry. When asked . . . what he looked for when hiring people, he answered: 'A breadth of knowledge about the world, rather than a narrow business school focus, and people who could write well, and discuss history and other subjects.' "[7]

Our participants concurred:

I still have that inquisitive nature. I collect rare books, wine, antiques; I do woodworking. It's a wide range of interests. I read a lot of books on the ancient world; I just finished a book on the Peloponnesian War and also The Rise and Fall of the Roman Empire. *(I admit, these are books that I should have read in college, but . . .) It's interesting how much we can learn from the ancient Greeks and Romans. I think that you need to round out the rough edges, but without losing the aggressiveness to lead change, to "become more wise without losing the fire."*

ഢ

What skills were the most important in my career? Broad grounding in the liberal arts, particularly philosophy, theology, and languages. This was particularly important at more senior levels but served as a fundamental underpinning of leadership throughout. Decisions

*must be made against some standard—an absolute, if you will—and
this standard becomes part of the leader's character.*

ᎧᏗ

*It's important for young people to read as many books as they can in
as wide a subject area as their interests will allow. Participate in
competitive sports and enjoy the competition.*

ᎧᏗ

A well-rounded person is as important as a brilliant person.

ᎧᏗ

*I gained a great deal of confidence from having achieved a higher
education at a good university. There are many early opportunities
to practice leadership: sports team captain, debating society, etc.
After the passing of the phase of the dot-com CEOs who were university dropouts, a solid, well-rounded education has become even more
relevant now.*

ᎧᏗ

*If possible, I'd suggest that young leaders seriously consider some grad-
uate education experience or at least ongoing formal educational
efforts to stay current in their chosen field and round out their people
skills. I've missed some of this as my family, business, and civic life have
continued to keep my life full. Perhaps if I had gotten some of this educational experience early on, it would have enhanced my total life.*

ᎧᏗ

*Get as broad a range of experience as possible; master professional
skills through exposure to as many areas as possible. This gives you
much more career flexibility. I'm in a technology position now, but
I'm not a technology person. When I was hired, my organization was
looking for someone who was good at processes.*

ᎧᏗ

*It's important not to lose sight of the big picture. We have a tendency
to focus solely on the issue at hand. That can be dangerous, because
the world changes very quickly. What's your top priority today may
not be tomorrow. To effectively anticipate and manage change, you
need a broad perspective.*

Choosing Your Battles

Many of our successful leaders stated how important it was for them to pick
their battles wisely, dealing with a few crucial issues and either delegating

the rest or saving the other issues for later. Managers who take on too much risk becoming exhausted by dealing with all the details.

In the early 1990s I became the CFO [chief financial officer] of my company's Japan operation. When I first started, there were about 22,000 Japanese employees, and I spoke no Japanese. It was initially a challenge of how to get things done, how to accomplish something. It forced me to adapt to the situation. I learned that you have to pick the important battles, not focusing on too many things. I didn't really learn this until I went to Asia. You can't sweat the small stuff.

ঔ৵৹

Only fight the battles that are "winnable." Choose your battles well.

ঔ৵৹

You can pick probably two or three battles, but you would get worn out if you tried to do it all. I gained a new appreciation for delegating to my staff.

Taking Smart Risks

A frequently mentioned leadership skill is the ability to take smart risks. A number of our participants cited this as something that is critical yet sometimes difficult to learn. When I asked several of our leaders if risk taking can be learned, they emphatically said yes. One participant said that many early-career leaders hesitate to take risks in making decisions, sometimes with good reason. He added that most companies encourage early-career, high-potential employees to take risks, telling them that "no one was ever killed here for taking a risk." Sounds good so far, but in fact there actually are consequences for "bad risks" in many companies. People do get fired or penalized for bad decisions. Employees know it, and so they don't get the practice they need in taking chances and making decisions.

It can depend on the organizational culture or on the manager himself or herself. But if you have a great track record or a halo effect, are on someone's radar, or have a good sponsor, you probably can take risks more easily than others can. This clearly correlates with Chapter 4 on mentoring: Mentors and sponsors identify the risks to take and help you navigate the sometimes tricky waters. However, the bottom line is that leaders must learn to take risks. Here are several observations from our participants:

One thing that is difficult for younger or less experienced people to learn is taking risks but not letting the risks you're taking slow you down. Just make the decision, then move on.

Take informed risks. I don't mean reckless ones. It helps you become visible—risk distinguishes people and companies. I think that risk can be learned. Some of it may be a tendency or capacity; part of it is in your heart. But you can learn to feel more comfortable with it. And assessing risk is as important as actually taking risks.

⌀⌀

Most of the world is gray. The decisions that leaders must make all include ambiguity. Leaders are confronted with problems without obvious solutions. Even after a decision is reached, you need to take prudent risks to implement that decision. Risk taking is crucial.

⌀⌀

I like to challenge my people with numbers. To improve performance, we agree on a goal that is difficult but feasible and publish the metrics. This isn't intended to embarrass anyone. Rather, I think it triggers a fire to excel in a person and brings out natural leadership qualities. I feel that you can unearth "hidden" leaders by exposing them to moderate risk. But it's a two-way street: I have to be willing to take the risk as well.

⌀⌀

Learn rapidly and fail fast. Always grow, be willing to take risks, and get beyond your failures quickly—expect disruptive events.

Other Important Leadership Characteristics

♦ Be prepared to take a chance on people even if they don't seem ready for the job yet. People must have felt they were taking a chance on you once.

♦ Be consistent, fair, and rational in your decision making or you will lose credibility. Try to get your team to do the same thing.

♦ Be aware of how acutely people pick up on your moods and any evidence of "divergence" from the norm they expect of you. They often read all sorts of things into this.

♦ Ask searching questions and get to agreed-upon actions with your people rather than just reeling off solutions or answers for them. This way, your people learn and get more confident because they work harder to get to the answers themselves.

♦ Live by the maxim "Confident people make for confident leaders."

OTHER RESEARCH ON LEADERSHIP DEVELOPMENT

The research studies described below examine and identify many of the skills that are increasingly necessary to today's leaders. Some of our participants have mentioned that their environment has changed significantly in the last fifteen to twenty years. Yet, interestingly enough, I don't believe that these skills have changed dramatically among the most successful leaders. For example, many generals and politicians throughout history displayed the skills of today's most forward-thinking leaders: communication, passion, caring about the team, and developing new leaders. However, I think that these themes have become more mainstream: More leaders can see their significance within the organization as well as with their customers.

To examine this evolution of leadership competencies and skills more closely, Andersen and the Finance Leadership Council at Motorola conducted a yearlong study of leadership development practices at nineteen organizations.[8] They wanted to identify effective ways to develop next-generation leadership as well as what kinds of environments encourage young leaders and how to measure their success.

The study found that leadership competencies seem to be similar across organizations, regardless of the industry. These competencies can create a common language for discussions about leadership development between managers and those who report to them: Everyone is on the same page. What was especially interesting was the emphasis on soft skills. Williams and Cothrel state, "The balance has clearly shifted from attributes traditionally thought of as masculine (strong decision-making, leading the troops, driving strategy, waging competitive battle) to more feminine qualities (listening, relationship-building and nurturing)."

What were some of these competencies across the nineteen organizations surveyed in this research study? Some of these competencies included the expected responses, such as delivering results, business literacy, and problem solving. However, a significant number of "soft skills" appeared in the research across industries, including building relationships, forming networks, being creative, and building teams. This reflects the results of our own research.

One of the participating companies, Levi Strauss & Co., shared its insights. As is true in many organizations, they realized that many of their leadership development decisions (who is outstanding, who should be given the opportunities) were the result of informal networks throughout the organization rather than a formal process. (This isn't news to most women. They already know that they're usually not part of these informal networks.)

Levi Strauss knew that its values needed to be more explicit, and so it developed the Aspirations Statement to identify its policies on diversity, teamwork, recognition, ethics, communication, and empowerment. The company also developed a formalized process of leadership development, transferring the primary emphasis on identifying potential leaders to the business unit leaders rather than the executive team; that made the previously somewhat "secretive" selection process more transparent and consensus-driven. It also allowed more nontraditional people with high potential to become more visible as candidates for leadership development opportunities.

A recent survey identified ten key competencies for leaders:[9]

- ♦ **Flexibility:** adapting to dynamic environments and thriving on change
- ♦ **Low risk aversion:** taking and managing risks to the organization's advantage
- ♦ **Business acumen:** knowing the industry trends and practices; understanding the competitors and the market environment
- ♦ **Vision:** leading with a vision of the future, not current trends; inspiring with a purpose
- ♦ **Ease with ambiguity and uncertainty:** the ability to act without having the total picture
- ♦ **Strategic agility:** seeing ahead and anticipating trends and consequences
- ♦ **Customer focus:** having a clear understanding of customers' needs and preferences
- ♦ **Communication:** relating to all levels of people, internal and external; the ability to build relationships
- ♦ **Motivation:** being charismatic and persuasive
- ♦ **Continuous learning:** analyzing successes and failures and learning from the experience

As you can see, although there are many different findings, depending on the study and its objectives, many commonalities appear. These various findings provide a comprehensive picture of the evolution of leadership development.

DEVELOPING YOUR OWN LEADERSHIP STYLE

Princeton University's Dr. Fred Greenstein, author of *The Presidential Difference: Leadership Style from FDR to Clinton,* gives the following advice to business leaders and others: "Study the performance of successful leaders in your field. Seek mentors. Be self-aware. Don't rest on your oars. Many American presidents lacked important skills when they were young, but went to great lengths to develop those skills. Leaders of industry should do the same."[10]

Many of our participants agreed. They suggested watching leaders you admire and modeling effective behavior after them. You should utilize mentoring opportunities, develop networking relationships, observe successful behavior, and adapt it to your specific needs and situations.

> *I would recommend to any aspiring leader to learn by watching others, leaders you respect. There's a chemistry; there's no substitute for that. You should always have your antenna up, thinking, What skills can I use? Keep your eyes open. There are many examples of success.*

> ∽

> *Earlier in my career I had a discussion with my boss about my leadership style. He said that I was "too soft." At first I was a little defensive, but I really did learn a lot about the best range of styles for me. It's interesting, too, that some of the early women in leadership positions in my company were not role models, since they had to take on male characteristics, but that is changing now. The organization encourages more balance, family, and community. A new role model is emerging for both men and women.*

> ∽

> *In terms of modeling, you end up as a patchwork quilt of experiences which you copy and learn . . . from individual bosses, from the culture of companies you work for, and from formal training. You adapt all this to your own style then, I think; it doesn't come across as credible or truthful if you just copy or regurgitate.*

> ∽

> *Trust your visceral reactions; use your intuition. There are seventy-five different ways to analyze an issue. Listen to your gut reactions.*

Potential leaders can approach the development of their leadership style systematically, asking themselves key questions regarding their leadership development needs. For example, many leaders realize that as they go higher in the organization, with hundreds or thousands of employees under them, the ability to set direction and delegate becomes more vital than team building and coaching. They realize that they need to adapt their communication style accordingly, and they identify a strategy to accomplish this. It is helpful to have a broad-based strategy for developing your leadership skills. In many of our programs we have discussed these issues. Try asking yourself the following questions:

- What are your key skills and competencies?
- Are there areas you would like to improve or develop? Which ones?
- What skills or competencies are valued at your organization? Do you exhibit them? If you don't know what is valued, who can tell you?
- Which leaders do you admire? Why? Have you established a professional relationship with them? If not, how can you do that? Networks? Professional associations? Volunteer opportunities?
- Do you show leadership outside the organization? How?
- Which leadership skills have you developed as a result? How do you plan to let others know about those skills?
- Have you developed a personal communication style that works for you? Do you change it from time to time? How? In what situations?
- Does your organization offer leadership development training? Is it available to everyone? If it is not, who will you identify as a mentor, coach, or sponsor to help you develop your leadership skills?
- What is your management or leadership style? Are you concerned with the bottom line or with human resources? Are you a charismatic leader, a visionary, or a change agent? How does that affect your chance of advancing in your organization?
- What are you good at? What are you known for? Managing people, managing projects, communicating the big picture, initiating start-up projects, fixing problems, or delivering what you say you will deliver?
- Does your style work with your boss? Your colleagues? Do you need to ask for feedback on your style?

WHAT DO FEMALE LEADERS BRING TO THE ORGANIZATION?

We have heard from many of our participants, both women and men, that women have added incredible richness to their organizations, especially in leadership roles. Much of what has been cited in the analysis of the new leadership style is, not coincidentally, the result of having women in more senior positions, and their male colleagues are the first to admit it.

I think that my leadership style has been modified by the different perspectives brought by several senior women within my organization. I also think that women's varied societal responsibilities bring a greater sensitivity to issues in the workplace. Having women in senior positions has helped to articulate the issues of managing a diverse workforce, bringing a balanced understanding rather than a mechanical approach to defining what motivates people.

∽

I have twelve vice presidents working for me, and nine are women. What do women bring to our organization? The sense that other things are important in life. And more compassion.

∽

I'm used to working with women in engineering, law, and finance. In my opinion, women have a better intuitive sense of others. They are more understanding of human emotion. They are critical in developing morale and loyalty. They know customers better than men do. They are more caring and more thoughtful about what others think. They connect emotionally, not just intellectually.

∽

In corporations, women bring positive values: They are 50 percent of the population, they provide insights, and you get a stronger company with different points of view, different approaches to problem solving.

What are the leadership strategies that women have utilized? They are largely the same as those used by any leader, but with a few keen perceptions added. Here is what some women have done to show their skills and competencies:

- ♦ **Establish your credibility as a leader.** Despite your credentials, don't assume that everyone knows what you've done.
- ♦ **Don't rest on your laurels.** What are you doing to build competencies, increase your visibility, take on new challenges, and develop key networks?
- ♦ **Be very well prepared and knowledgeable when you go into meetings or negotiations.** Don't leave any room for doubt.
- ♦ **Work even harder.** In assessments of competence, women are often held to a different standard, and so they have to work harder and better in order to be recognized.

At its annual conference, Catalyst presented the results of its study of women in corporate leadership in which female executives attributed their success to the following factors:

- Consistently exceeding expectations
- Developing a style with which male managers are comfortable
- Seeking out difficult assignments
- Having an influential mentor

It is interesting that education can level the playing field somewhat, at least in corporations. Women who earn a master of business administration degree cut the salary disparity between themselves and their male counterparts in half.[11]

WHAT WOULD I HAVE DONE DIFFERENTLY, OR WHAT DO I DO DIFFERENTLY NOW?

We asked our participants what they would have done differently. Some said, "Actually, probably nothing. I think I was lucky to get a lot of advice and do the right things." But a number of our participants shared what they would do differently if they were to do it again.

When asked what he would have done differently, one respondent said, "Get a good grounding in financials and be able to read a balance sheet." He decided in his midtwenties that if he was going to move up in the organization with an economics degree, he was going to need a stronger financial background. He went back to school for an accounting certification. Another British executive agreed. With a prestigious degree in a humanities discipline, he realized that he needed a solid financial background. It was helpful to be able to interpret the financial data and understand the red flags and to ask valid questions about the data.

Although it was not essential, many senior executives have mentioned the same thing: Some kind of formal or informal mentoring, certification, degree, or experience is very helpful, especially if you're in a nonfinance area such as human resources, corporate communications, or marketing.

Several executives also mentioned that getting an international posting would have helped, rather than just traveling internationally. This would have greatly prepared them for a more global environment. Another executive commented on the importance of seeing "the big picture":

Probably the two things I do most differently now are, first, resist the temptation to get too involved at the detail level. Second, I try to pick three or four themes and keep reinforcing them in the business so that I get identified as an individual with some tangible assets.

SUMMARY
Success Secret #9: Develop Key Leadership Skills

♦ Deliver results all the time—consistently.

♦ Practice making decisions. No matter what the decision is, move on once you've made it.

♦ Listen to the people you lead.

♦ Keep your ego in check.

♦ Be passionate about what you believe in and share that passion.

♦ Be curious about a broad range of things.

♦ Choose your battles.

♦ Develop a comfort level with risk.

♦ Become well rounded.

♦ Develop a leadership style that works for you.

For a list of research participants, please see page xvii.

Develop the Next Generation of Leaders

⚓

I was past forty when I came onto the serious leadership track. I was in operations and was content to be there. I had a mentor who thought that "maybe this guy can do more." This is where the cross-development came into play. He sent me to Latin America and Asia, and I also gained experience in sales and marketing. There were several times when he pressed buttons, telling me that I was doing a good job, but he also said, "You can do better." He had to take some risks in promoting me; there was always the chance that I would fail.

There is a specific reason why I chose the opening quote for this chapter. Many of us think that when we talk about developing the next generation of leaders, we are referring only to early-career young people. However, as you will see, "the next generation" means simply that: the people coming up behind existing leaders. I really want to emphasize that point. We are talking not only about those with high potential right out of college or graduate school but about people at all levels. Think about it. Who is in line for the position of senior vice president of operations or chief financial officer? People who are already well into their careers. They presumably already know many of the strategies necessary to advance their careers, but they still need to develop the specific new skills required for the next position. What we are talking about is a *process* of leadership development. I'm talking about the twenty-five-year-old first-time manager or team leader, the forty-five-year-old vice president in line for the chief financial officer position, and the fifty-seven-year-old executive who wants to start her own company and sit on corporate boards. There are potential leaders at every level of the organization, and the same process applies to all of them.

DEVELOPING LEADERS AT EVERY LEVEL

What are the elements of this leadership development process? Potential leaders are people who have the basic skills and potential for the position but need a sponsor or advocate to recommend them to the right people and a mentor to show them the ropes and give them advice. They need someone who is willing to take a chance on them, someone who will introduce them to the right people in the network and give them broader opportunities and responsibilities so that they can prove themselves.

Keep this process in mind as you read the examples and quotes in this chapter. You may be gathering information for your own early career, as a means to make your next management move, or even as a way to set organizational policy by benchmarking what other organizations have done. There undoubtedly will be observations and experiences that will relate to you regardless of your position or age.

Here's an example. A few years ago I gave a dinner keynote address to the National Association of Women Legislators, a nonpartisan group that identifies and selects high-potential women in politics for an intensive week of workshops, training, and coaching. When they asked me to speak, I thought, What the heck I am going to teach these women about how to be successful? I'd say they are already there. But it was fascinating. Many of them shared their experiences of the week with me. Among many other things, they had worked with a communications expert who gave them information on persuasive speaking, participating effectively in political debates, dealing with the media, and communicating in a crisis. They practiced their on-camera skills with television-taping workshops. They also developed new networks and shared their experiences with their colleagues. They identified potential mentors and sponsors to show them the ropes. They all agreed that these were specific skills required in their positions and were wonderfully targeted to their needs.

We also talked about their career paths and goals: Had they prepared themselves to be, or even seen themselves, as leaders? I asked them, "How many of you have planned specifically for this position? How many of you even thought five years ago that you would be here right now?" They laughed, and only about 10 percent raised their hands. They admitted that this was new territory for them as first-time leaders. And believe me, most of them were not kids. They were mature, experienced, talented women in their thirties, forties, and fifties.

We talked about how this move into politics had affected their families and their senses of personal time and balance. We also talked about their future plans and goals, things that most of them hadn't thought about.

How were they going to parlay this experience into the next move? Go into corporations or higher education? Become members of boards? What were the skills and competencies that they could transfer to the next move? They really enjoyed doing this exercise, which allowed them to reflect and to identify the skills they needed to work on as they advanced in their careers.

It is very helpful to identify one or several people to help you with your career goals, both short-term and long-term. Keep in mind that you may be in a position to help the next generation as well. Here is one leader's example:

> *I have tried to work with people to determine what their career aspirations were. Sometimes people are not showing leadership skills because they are early in their career and are not fully engaged in the work they are doing. I find they are often talented people with a great deal of potential but seem to be simply going through the motions: doing whatever they are assigned, sometimes taking it to the next level but not really being fully engaged by projects or assignments. I have sometimes found that this type of employee lacks a clear focus or path, which is not unusual for people early in their careers. I work with these highly talented people and try to help them develop some short- and long-term goals and find ways to achieve those goals. Sometimes that includes transitioning off my team when they realize that working for me helps achieve a short-term goal but not the long-term goal. And if this is the case, that's fine. On the other hand, it sometimes works out that they realize there is a career path in our organization and maybe being on my team will help them achieve both long-term career and personal goals.*

As you read on, put yourself into the examples and quotes. I guarantee that they apply to you.

HELPING EVERYONE IN THE ORGANIZATION BECOME A LEADER

We have been hearing this consistently across industries: *Everyone in the organization needs to develop leadership skills and behaviors.* People need to be able to analyze information, make decisions, take risks, and build relationships. Leadership guru Noel Tichy adds, "The best-led companies are the ones that develop leaders throughout the organization. And potential leaders are embedded in every level—if only an organization's leaders can spot them. . . . [Leadership] characterized by the ability to teach and learn from a wide variety of people . . . is actually better suited to the everyday challenges of running a business."[1]

Here is what some of our leaders had to say:

There are many technically competent managers who come late to leadership. It is the organization's responsibility to provide values to encourage these leaders: clarity of direction, honesty, trust. Recognize that there are different leaders for different purposes and give individuals permission to develop leadership capabilities. Most people have some leadership potential, but it needs to be encouraged and nurtured. For those who are more introverted, you need to create an organizationally safe environment to build their confidence.

ᴄᐧᐧᐤ

Leaders are found not only at the top of the organization. Your consultants can show leadership in projects, programs, technology, recruiting others into the business. . . . The common thread? Groom leaders early; everyone participates.

ᴄᐧᐧᐤ

People are leaders if they are cultivating others. They accept leadership responsibility early in their careers, as quickly as they can. In addition, they must look out for and train those coming up behind them. There's a learning curve: You learn quickly, implement it, then teach it to others. Leadership is used often: You nurture it, take care of others' learning, help those behind you. Learning includes

- *Technology*
- *Industry knowledge (clients, environment, etc.)*
- *Leadership skills*

This is what we use in developing leadership.

ᴄᐧᐧᐤ

A recommendation to leaders looking to the next generation: "Go beyond your immediate circle, to places where you've never been in the organization, and ask around: Who has made a difference? Who thinks differently? Who comes from a different background?"[2]

Discovering Dormant Leaders

We've been talking about teaching everyone in the organization to be a leader. Most senior executives agree that it's pretty easy to spot the top 10 to 20 percent of employees who have high potential. But many of them also discuss the challenges of identifying the less visible employees who have not yet emerged. Many employees have certain skills or talents that have not yet been identified, even by the employees themselves. It may take a catalyst to bring these skills to the forefront, a specific situation in which a person rises to the challenge.

In the military you never know where your leaders are going to come from. In a battle, the captain is killed, the sergeant isn't up to the task, so it's the eighteen-year-old farm kid from Iowa who takes the lead.[3]

✧

There is management potential lurking among your sales and marketing staff, even if you don't see it on a day-to-day basis. The difficult part is identifying latent talent among employees who aren't usually responsible for management duties. In sales organizations, it's been quite traditional to promote the best salesperson to manager, instead of thinking, "What do we need in a manager to maximize the effectiveness of the sales team?" . . . The clear thinking, planning and project management skills used in sales are the same ones that make for good managers, but these skills are used in different ways. More than anything, you need to find people who have the desire to manage others, not just their own projects.[4]

The author Debra Meyerson agrees: "Everyday leaders often fail to show up on the radar screen because they occupy the lower echelons of the organization chart or work in very quiet ways. Some advance an agenda of social responsibility—environmentalism, gender equity, or diversity, for example. But there are also people who advance product innovations, who want to make the workplace more creative in an organization that feels oppressive. They struggle with how much they can rock the boat and at the same time stay inside of it and get ahead."[5]

Organizations tend to classify their people according to their technical capabilities. Traditionally, leaders have been identified by giving someone a problem. If he or she can't do it, give it to the next guy. Although individuals must take responsibility for themselves, it's important to give employees the tools to develop self-awareness. Leaders can wake up dormant potential leaders by showing them where they stand in the organization.

Several of our leaders shared their experiences:

If, for example, your corporate goal is to provide great customer service, decision-making capabilities need to be moved down through the organization. If you are clear about what's expected, people will rise to the challenge.

⠂⠄⠂

I believe in overcoming any kind of bias by providing the same train-ing and experience opportunities for all potential leaders. If you cre-ate an opportunity for people to succeed, the cream really will rise to the top. You can't create diversity by simply bringing someone in to fill a slot at a higher level. You need to start the effort at the entry level, with equal opportunities to excel through training.

⠂⠄⠂

I was fortunate to have the opportunity to learn leadership skills while "a big fish in a little pond." I was in the number-two position in a small subsidiary of a large organization. I was able to benefit from the experience of how large organizations worked and what part politics played, for example, but was still in a position to make significant decisions in the small unit.

Motivating Nonleaders

The truth is, for all our discussions about everyone in the organization's ability to lead, not everyone can lead at the same level. Not everyone has the skill, the intellectual capacity, the drive, the interest, and the motivation. But that doesn't mean that we don't want everyone in the organization to be an outstanding contributor. The trick is to help find each person's strength and capitalize on it.

A friend of mine, John, an experienced manager, looks for the unique skill in each person and publicly compliments him or her on it. One of the people who reports to him, for example, loves information: He is an avid reader and Internet surfer, and so he constantly brings in articles and infor-mation that he knows his boss needs. John doesn't have much time for doing this, and he loves having short summaries or articles to peruse. In front of others, John says things like, "Wow, you keep me really up to date on these topics. I would never have the time to find all this great informa-tion. I really appreciate it." His employee has no interest in leading teams or being considered for the fast track, but he knows that he adds a lot of value to his team and to his boss. He is contributing to the bottom line in his own way by providing data.

The important thing is to choose one or two things and excel at them. My older brother, for example, is very intellectual and has a nearly photo-graphic memory, but he is not athletic. In high school he tried out for the baseball team without success. The coach realized that his skill lay else-where; he became the well-respected and well-liked team manager and proudly wore his letter sweater. Still a huge sports fan, he has compensated for his lack of physical skill with his incredible wealth of knowledge, remembering just about every statistic and interesting bit of information on most teams, especially in baseball. The message? If you can't be the superstar leader of the team, that doesn't mean you can't be an outstanding contributor.

One of our participants shared his company's philosophy, which is the same strategy my brother follows: You don't have to be an expert in every-thing; just choose one thing and be as good at it as you can be.

What if they don't have potential? Our company gives you two years to develop a leadership signature. They expect people to be good at something. Some people are good at everything, but not most. Think of kids at school: If you're at the bottom of everything, it's very demoralizing. But if you're good at just one thing, you have a better self-image. Pick one thing and do it well. Don't work on rounding out many areas of weakness; develop one skill aggressively. You need to be outstanding only in one or two things.

ల⌀ు

A successful leader has a combination of knowledge and experience. It is an acquired skill. But not everyone wants to be a leader, and an organization should provide an alternative path to success to accom-modate talent without staff management or leadership responsibil-ity. Once again, it's a matter of finding out what motivates people and trying to give it to them.

ల⌀ు

In the baby boom generation and earlier generations there has been the idea that if you work hard enough, you can be the President of the United States. I think that this has changed. I tell people that you don't need to run the company. Sometimes high achievers are devas-tated when they find out that they can't, but I tell people, "Figure out what makes you happy. Reassess what you want to do." A lot of them have children, families. There are sacrifices you have to make to run a big company—for some it's worth it; for some it's not. Where does your career fit in your life? I see this as a frustration for my daughter and her friends who are about to graduate from college. They're fac-ing the questions of career, balance, "what am I going to do with my life?" I also see it with colleagues who are in the next tier of their careers—the challenges they face. If you're offered a job with a lot more money but it will make you miserable, what do you do? You really have to understand the idea of balance.

Several leaders mentioned the importance of offering incentives and providing motivation and positive reinforcement to employees as a key factor in bringing out the best in *all* workers.

It's a challenge for probably every CEO: how to get the best out of average performers. Every year we recruit thousands of students, mostly on campuses, and usually talk to the top 10 percent of the graduating class. Probably about 10 to 15 percent are leaders, about 65 percent are average to good, and the others are usually moving in and out of the organization. The leaders are going to move up anyway, but how do you motivate the others? Superior compensation based on performance is one way, especially in a great market economy. But sharing the passion and excitement with the employees is also important. You have to keep up your own level of passion. Your employees need to understand their critical role in the organization.

∾

Fundamentally, "geeks" are interested in having an impact. They believe in their ideas, and they like to win. If you don't want to lose your geeks, you have to find a way to give them promotions without turning them into managers. Most of them are not going to make very good executives, and in fact, most of them would probably turn out to be terrible managers. But you need to give them a forward career path, you need to give them recognition, and you need to give them more money.[6]

∾

Be attentive to how the different generations in your firm are motivated. Develop dynamic reward systems that respond to the changing needs of your workforce. But spend most of your time fostering values that create networks of cooperation. The key elements here include the willingness to help others, the acceptance of personal responsibility for outcomes, and a bias for action.[7]

Attracting and Retaining High-Potential Leaders

A study published in 2000 by McKinsey & Co. projected that in fifteen years the demand for talented employees between the ages of thirty-five and forty-five will increase by about 25 percent. What can the chief executive officer (CEO) do to make sure his or her company attracts and retains the best of the best?[8]

I hear this issue mentioned frequently when I talk to corporations. Many of the participants in our research cited the critical need to attract talent to their organizations, and most said that there is a marked shortage of leaders. They want people who can think critically, analytically, and strategically; communicate; lead teams; and take the initiative. However, unlike in the past, when workers with specific degrees or experiences were sought out solely by companies in that field, many companies are competing for the same people—the skill set is readily transferable. The pharmaceutical companies, for example, are competing for talent not only with other pharmaceutical companies but with many other industries as well.

What do high-potential workers look for in organizations? We hear many of the usual things: the reputation of the organization, the type of work, interesting work, opportunities for advancement, challenge, salary. But "compared to their older colleagues, the cubicle set (those under 30) are significantly more likely to say they want a CEO who motivates and inspires them. But they want more than a mission statement, company logo and coffee mug—they want an experience. These newcomers want to be told and shown why they should work for you and how they can contribute."[9]

Royal Dutch Shell has developed an innovative opportunity for employees with high potential to gain that experience. They invite young employees with leadership potential to join several teammates from other parts of the world for a six-month assignment designed to "create value" for the company. Four teams operate simultaneously with various goals, all under the sponsorship of a company-provided coach. At the end of the project each team presents its recommendations to senior management, which decides whether to accept or reject that proposal. Of course, this assignment does not preclude their own work, and so the participants say that it forces one to learn how to delegate, but they agree that it's an extraordinary opportunity for personal growth. However, the company also benefits from the program. If the recommendations are accepted, Shell has an enviable opportunity to gain insight into future trends through the eyes of its future leaders.[10]

Our participants agreed that a dynamic, challenging work environment is crucial in attracting and retaining high-potential employees:

We brought forty to sixty people, high potentials, to an off-site meeting and introduced a real-life problem or issue, like growing a part of the business. They worked together in small groups, discussed strate-

gies, and came up with solutions. I spent the entire day with them and had the opportunity to see them in action. We used this program model for four or five years, and now we have created the "next generation," in which younger potential leaders come together for two or three months to work on issues. Various satellites have developed, and it has now become part of the culture for leadership development.

ᴄᴧᴎᴦ

I was fortunate to have the opportunity to practice leadership at MCI, where I joined the "start-up" company with fewer than 200 employees and stayed through its evolution into a multi-billion-dollar organization. The founder, Bill McGowan, was the personification of a leader. He attracted top talent. He picked people with certain skills—the ability to execute, the ability to build relationships, the "care factor"—and sent those people into new experiences. He knew that if they had the fundamentals, they could learn the rest. Bill put them into experiences above their heads but coached them through it. I learned not to rely too much on formal "management development" courses. Gaining experience counts.

ᴄᴧᴎᴦ

Establish a dialogue—a safety net—asking subordinates questions about why they want to do a particular thing. Help them reach their own conclusions without giving them the answer. If an employee comes in and asks, "Should I take this risk?" ask, "What are the implications, what are the benefits, what's the downside? What's the worst-case scenario?" Let them come up with their own conclusions. I give feedback to employees: Have they thought it through enough? Are they prepared enough? What do they still need to work on? Without giving them my answers, I let them come up with their own.

THE IMPORTANCE OF EARLY LEADERSHIP EXPERIENCE

In addition, many of our participants suggested that employees get leadership experience as early as possible. Ask your mentor or sponsor for help in identifying leadership opportunities—and do a great job! Practice leadership skills in as many situations as possible, not only at work. A number of them also mentioned that they are more closely examining their leadership selection processes, initiatives, mentoring and development opportunities, and sponsorship, and are giving high-potential leaders more opportunities to stretch themselves by taking on more responsibility at a younger age. It's important to get a lot of experience as early as you can. You must realize that some decisions will work and others won't, but you will learn from each experience, each mistake, and each project.

I would give the same advice to anyone that I give to my own kids and that my parents gave to me. Don't lose sight of opportunities to develop your leadership skills. Give back to those who have less than you do. Get involved in community activities. My daughter has been involved in community activities, working in soup kitchens and leading a group of people to raise money to clean up parks and neighborhoods. Some of these leadership opportunities are overlooked.

ல்

Young leaders must perform a balancing act. It's a case of being interesting versus being interested. You want to create a good impression, but you have to be prepared to contribute good ideas for the success of your team. Earn the respect of your colleagues by strengthening the team, not by trying to be the shining star at their expense. It's sometimes a challenge for young people to create that fusion of good ideas to achieve a win-win situation.

ல்

To make decisions in the proper context, you must have actually done it all yourself. A formal business education teaches students how to analyze but not how to motivate and lead. Potential leaders need to focus early on learning leadership.

ல்

I'd advise future generations to take leadership roles early in their lives and to have empathy for people. Service in the armed forces, the Peace Corps, or other government, public service, or nonprofit positions can often offer leadership opportunities at a younger age than can working in larger corporate environments.

As we discussed earlier, mentoring and support from senior staff members is an excellent way to gain early leadership experience.

We are in the process of instituting Six Sigma in our company. We are just picking our "black belts" now. This will give them the early leadership experience to propel them upward. The young sometimes fall down in leadership performance. This will give them a chance to gain additional project management training, in addition to their technical training.

◦\⌐

In my organization I wanted to get a more diverse environment, especially in higher positions, and so I decided to identify promising, high-potential women and minorities. I felt that the fastest way for young people to learn leadership was to rotate high potentials every four months and take them everywhere—into key meetings as long as they weren't confidential, to company events with the governor. Everywhere I went, they went. They were exposed to situations and experiences they never would have had. Five of the seventeen participants in this program ultimately became officers in this company, two of whom are women. They largely credit this exposure for their success.

◦\⌐

Very often executive assistants are picked as high-flying individuals with lots of potential, those who can provide one-on-one support to a very senior executive and, in doing so, gain some really high-quality fast-track development. Sometimes they don't necessarily capitalize on the opportunity in terms of ensuring that some of the things they want to get out of the role were explicit at the start (because this might be seen to be, horror of horrors, pushy).

I would advise the people reading this to pursue opportunities to work alongside both male and female senior people in a mentoring/ supporting capacity whenever they can. But in doing so, be really professional about it; that means being clear about what your side of the bargain is regarding learning, development, and the next steps. Don't be afraid of being clear about this and engaging in debate at the beginning of your contracted period. Taking on this issue is a sign not of being aggressive but of being assertive. It reinforces the reasons you have been asked to do that sort of job in the first place.

Learning to Lead

Keep in mind that while most of these leaders recommend getting leadership experience as early as possible, many senior people are concerned about the next generation's lack of exposure to leadership development opportunities. In the past, many early-career to midcareer people—future leaders of organizations—had already experienced a number of leadership opportunities before they started their work careers, most often in sports or military environments. But many leaders in diverse industries, most with different backgrounds, have repeated the same message: How do we give the next generation of leaders the opportunity to develop their leadership skills?

Researchers increasingly have found that many young people have developed a high level of technology expertise but that some do not realize the importance of the business side of things: dealing with people, working effectively in teams, communicating, taking the initiative. However, this is not necessarily a trait of a specific generation; it is more a matter of professional immaturity.

A number of our participants shared their experiences, especially with regard to leading teams and projects. As we mentioned in Chapter 3, these leaders specified how high potentials took on a project, completed it successfully, gained visibility, and were given further responsibility—in other words, they took the opportunity to develop leadership skills. What are some of the leadership skills required in organizations today? As we mentioned earlier, many of them are integral to project management: the ability to develop effective teams, to bring people together to consensus, and to communicate effectively both by giving clear direction and by listening to team members. These leaders added that often it can be helpful to take on the projects no one else wants and do them very well.

However, they also highlighted a far-too-common occurrence among employees—the considerable percentage of their workforce that displays a professional immaturity with regard to leadership, regardless of their age. Many of today's managers are having to teach basic communication and team-building skills to employees before the employees can take on their first projects, and this is clearly a frustration to busy managers. In addition, many early-career employees often fail to take required initiative—they wait to be told what to do. We heard this one a lot from executives across industries! (They hold responsible the MTV/computer game mentality in which people are passive observers rather than active participants. Many of these employees have never learned to take initiative.) These employees may often feel that merely trying hard is the most important thing—rather than a successful outcome. They do not take responsibility for their actions. They may frequently expect the company or their boss to take charge of their career management. They do not provide solutions or recommendations during project meetings; they simply present data, statistics, or a problem that needs to be solved. Many feel that their extraordinary technical skills take precedence over the need for basic business or leadership skills—that their technology expertise is enough.

Again, keep in mind that this is not necessarily a trait of the younger generation; you probably have experienced it many times with people of all ages. I know that I have.

One of our participants gave his advice:

If you aspire to rise through an organization, I would suggest "thinking like your boss." What are the issues on his or her desk? Look at what needs to be taken care of and start assessing solutions yourself. Take action now rather than waiting until you're given that position.

A study adds, "Technical skills are necessary, but not sufficient for promotion in some organizations. Business skills and people skills are also required. The largest factor contributing to the failure by technical managers is that they do not possess the people skills needed to manage others. Suggestions for increasing promotion opportunities include more networking . . . as well as being technically competent."[11]

I agree. For example, I have worked with new managers who say, "I'm in technology, and that's one of the reasons why I chose this field. I prefer dealing with computers to dealing with people. I'm not a people person, and I hate the thought of managing people." But I've also talked to a lot of experienced managers in technology who have moved up in their organizations. I ask them if they have had to work on their communication skills. Many of them laugh and say, "I didn't think that I would have to, but now I have to make presentations all the time, work with teams, work with people at all levels of the organization."

It is critical to understand the importance of learning the basic skills of business despite your background or major in school—there's a lot more to it than content expertise. If you're working on a project, you have to learn to deal with people. Give clear directions to the team members. Listen to their concerns. If you are faced with a problem, take the initiative—don't wait to be told what to do. People skills are essential.

Some of our participants offered their perspectives on and personal experiences with developing talent and advancing in an organization.

For the first time in my career I had to manage a big team. My strong points are finance and technology—I could often work independently. I didn't really like dealing with people's issues. What I needed was a lot of help in communication.

ᘯ

We send the top 10 percent of employees to our corporate "business school" to learn the overall picture of the company. You can tell after twelve weeks who will be good. As the CEO, I teach a two-hour course during the program, and I can already start to pick out the leaders by the end of the course.

♧

There's a lack of loyalty today. Many younger people need to pay their dues. They need to earn what they get. A lot of them have good technical skills, but many don't have the people skills.

What are you supposed to do if you haven't graduated from a military academy or another leadership training ground in which to learn early leadership skills? As we said before, it has become more and more important for potential leaders at all levels to identify mentors, advocates, or sponsors to help them navigate the sometimes tricky waters of leadership development. Those people can help you identify leadership opportunities and help you manage risk. They can give you advice and feedback. Broaden your support and information network. Be a sounding board in tough and challenging situations.

It is critical for next-generation leaders of all ages to pay attention to good advice. Many mentors or advocates encourage developing a strong skill set and also taking smart risks. Success in higher-risk projects can distinguish high-potential people.

Strive to have varied assignments throughout your career. Organizations want leaders who have a broad background.

♧

You don't need to work 100 percent harder to get more results. Often you can just work 10 percent harder—and smarter—to get 100 percent more results. If others work forty hours a week, you don't necessarily need to work eighty hours—often forty-five or fifty is good. It's what you do with the time that matters.

♧

What can you do to get noticed? Sit in for someone at a meeting; find new ways of doing things. Don't just talk about an idea at a meeting; spend some time and energy presenting a completed project idea. This is important to do while you're young to enhance your image and increase visibility. Find something that's never been done, read industry information outside your area, and learn about the whole company, not just your area.

♧

Grow where you're planted. The younger generations are very upwardly mobile, with an eye on the next level. Consequently, they don't necessarily do a great job in their current positions. It's very important to balance the two and not focus purely on what's next. Always do the best job that you can.

THE CHANGING FACE OF CAREER DEVELOPMENT: LEADING GENERATION X

There is no doubt that the overall environment and perspectives of work are changing dramatically. New themes are emerging: flexibility, quality of work, the work environment itself—less formal in dress, attitudes, behavior, chain of command. A clear flow of communication is important. Balance and quality of life are also concerns. These issues are of particular interest to younger workers, though they are increasingly relevant to people of all ages.

One of our senior executives agreed. He shared his personal philosophy, and he's not a Gen Xer!

In terms of balance, don't forget that you have a life outside of work. People who are totally dedicated to work can become too narrow. They need to be able to put things in perspective to be successful in their professional lives.

"Younger workers generally tend not to show the workaholic tendencies characteristic of most baby boomers; they seem to think that boomers also take themselves too seriously. How do you deal with the differences in characteristics between the two generations? Remember, Gen Xers have been raised in a different world: They want clear information about their responsibilities and goals, more informal dress codes, more flexibility, less hierarchy, and the freedom to do the job their own way."[12]

"This generation is used to globalization, downsizing, changing authority roles, and the technology revolution, which keeps them more in sync with today's workplace. Be prepared to coach, cajole, and negotiate, but demand the moon and the stars in return."[13]

There is not one stereotype of younger workers. Many high-flying MBAs do not fit the image of the laid-back Gen Xer who fails to take the initiative. They want to make an impact, and fast. Yes, they're looking for interesting jobs with flexibility and excitement, but they also want a chance to work on high-profile assignments with a lot of exposure outside their functional areas. In a *Fortune* article,[14] top MBAs cite the specific qualities that they look for in an ideal employer:

♦ Good references for my future career

♦ Competitive compensation

- Exciting products and services
- A variety of tasks or assignments
- Immediate responsibility
- A dynamic organization
- A strong corporate culture
- International and relocation possibilities
- Likable, inspiring colleagues

How can you meet the needs of younger workers? I've talked to many young, early-career workers who are clear on their needs. Many say that they want to be heard. They want to be valued. They want to have interesting, meaningful work and job flexibility. They want to maximize their technical skills, their problem-solving skills, their creative, outside-the-box approaches to issues. They are comfortable with the unknown. They are more concerned with results than "face time," the time actually spent on the job. They want variety—different types of projects and tasks.

Yet, my actual experience with Gen Xers in the workplace has been mixed. I keep going back to the different things I have heard about leadership: The top 10 percent are great, the next 20 percent are pretty good, the middle 50 percent are average, and the others haven't made it yet. In corporate seminars I see dozens of outstanding young leaders who are motivated, success-oriented, and highly skilled. They're really amazing and great to be around. They are probably the 5 to 10 percent of this population who have graduated from excellent schools and have been prepared for success and leadership from an early age. There are also the young technology experts—maybe another 5 to 10 percent. They are highly intelligent and innovative, and their performance and outstanding skills are difficult to ignore. Then there's the big average group. But that leaves a pretty sizable percentage of this generation who are unfortunately ill prepared for the workplace and may be in for a rude awakening when they begin their careers. I have seen it frequently, and so have many of my colleagues: young people who fail to take initiative or who want to start in the "ideal job" but lack the skills essential for that job.

Most of our readers in this generation undoubtedly fall into the first category. Why else would you be reading a book on developing leadership skills? Well prepared, skilled, and intelligent, you probably are on track for success and are looking for a reasonable amount of advice and guidance. However, many of your peers and team members—regardless of age—do not have your skill, motivation, and drive. As team leaders you will be dealing with these issues. Your success, your visibility, and your image will be reflected in the effectiveness of your team—and your team leadership. Don't underestimate this responsibility. It is in your best interest to hone your skills in communication and team building to motivate your team members to do their best. You will need to earn their respect and trust. At an early stage you often will be called upon as a guide, giving advice on team strategies and behavior. Talk to your own mentors and advocates to get their advice on maximizing team success, motivation strategies, keeping your team focused, and gaining personal and team visibility and recognition.

Life as a project manager revolves around managing surprises and making trade-offs. If you don't aggressively, tangibly, and visibly manage your time in your organization, you're history. . . . This is a great time to be a young person in business. Focus and fearlessness are what count. This company is full of Generation X people who simply don't know that the technologies they're using "don't work." They want the jobs nobody else wants. That's what's cool.[15]

∽

Get some experience in project management. For example, our company has about three years of projects ready to go. There are unlimited opportunities—many situations where no one wants the job. It's a good chance to shine. Success on smaller projects leads to bigger teams.

ADVICE FROM THE EXPERTS

Leadership coach Ram Charan talks about the three crucial passages in moving up the leadership ladder in today's businesses with flatter hierarchies, describing when a manager should ask for help.

First, the transition from managing yourself to managing others. Despite the urge to keep on doing "the stuff you love," first-time managers must learn how to plan, assign work, motivate, and evaluate.

The second transition is from managing others to being a functional manager. This is the first time that you will be leading people in disciplines outside your own experience and expertise. Before, you were the best practitioner; now you must become the best listener and learn how your function fits into the overall plan of the business. You are no longer managing projects, you're helping put the company in a stronger strategic position.

Finally, the transition from managing a function to managing a business—this is the big one. The biggest adjustment is learning to evaluate a course of action not just in terms of functionality (can we do it?), but in terms of profitability over time (should we do it?).

It's at these three points that people are most likely to need help— a manager ought to get guidance from coursework, coaches, and a closely attentive boss.[16]

Young leaders—or future leaders—must remember what their bosses are looking for: results, performance, and team leadership. Many of our participants said that success on early projects or in team leadership is what they first notice in young people with high potential. This is their opportunity to shine. If they do well here, they will be assigned bigger projects and be given a chance to prove their abilities. Organizations are desperate for leaders. If you need advice or guidance on what you should be doing, find several mentors, advocates, coaches, and sponsors. They will be critical in the development of your leadership potential.

♦ Be yourself. Do what works best for you rather than modeling your style after others you see as successful.

♦ Balance your experience between staff and line responsibilities.

♦ Seek early experiential learning situations.

♦ Practice leadership in situations with less potential impact on your career or the organization, where deficiencies aren't as obvious.

♦ Be sure that you really do want a leadership role. Not everyone has the skill and/or desire to become a good leader.

It's important for emerging leaders to take a hand in managing their own careers.

Leadership tends to be viewed as "you either have it or you don't." I don't agree. You can take courses, read books—it can even be self-taught. Young people seem to focus on substantive knowledge but don't appreciate that without leadership skills, it's wasted. Everything that we do in corporations is based on teams; it's multidisciplinary, bringing people together, creating critical mass.

⌘

Early in your career, don't hesitate to move around to other companies. It will help broaden your experience and accelerate your career advancement.

Managing others is the perfect opportunity to begin to gain leadership experience and valuable management skills.

Early on you need to get into a position to supervise something. Also, get varied experiences—not only workplace-based. Look for other opportunities to get transferable experience (the Jaycees, for example).

ϡ

You need to make a commitment to support people once you've taken a chance on them—and provide feedback. There is a critical obligation to the next generation to provide information and guidance. In my own experience I have found it helpful when I am in a difficult situation to think, How would so-and-so have handled this? I have tried to figure out who was doing this well and mirror them.

ϡ

I would encourage more junior leaders to gain experience in situations with less potential impact on both the organization and their own careers. This is when deficiencies are less obvious. I've seen too many managers get their first shot at leadership when they're placed two levels of responsibility higher than they should have been.

Other qualities helpful for leaders are breadth of experience in the industry or company and a healthy sense of competition.

When talking about management development, make sure that people have multiple experiences. There are about ten of us who are in senior management, and although it's not necessarily written down, we've all had similar experiences: various functions, overseas assignments, etc.

ϡ

Of course, you need business skills, people skills, and other appropriate leadership skills. But competition is still a very important part of the business model, the sports model, for example. This whole competitiveness—beating the other guy, they're trying to get our customers, competing with technology. You just have to know the balance.

SUMMARY

Success Secret #10: Develop the Next Generation of Leaders

♦ Leaders are found everywhere in organizations—across functions and at all levels.

♦ Everyone needs to be a leader—at different times and in different situations.

♦ As a leader, seek out potential leaders and identify strategies to maximize the productivity and satisfaction of those who can't or don't want to lead.

♦ Develop strategies to attract and retain talent.

♦ People skills are necessary for leadership.

♦ Understand the perspectives and motivations of different generations of leaders.

For a list of research participants, please see page xvii.

Conclusion

One of the interesting things I've noticed since we did the research for our first book five years ago is the evolution of women in organizations. What was it like for women ten or fifteen years ago in organizations—women who wanted to get ahead and achieve parity? The primary emphasis was on *what organizations could do for them*, and, believe me, there was a lot that needed to be done. Organizations were largely an old boys' network in the mid-1980s and early 1990s, and most of the research and buzz focused on work-life balance, building networks, establishing mentoring programs, and encouraging diversity initiatives. Women were at the forefront of encouraging change, largely at the organizational level rather than at the individual level, working with senior management in creating these initiatives and presenting data to establish "women's programs" and flexible work schedules. In the middle to late 1990s things started to change. A lot of organizations (some more enthusiastically than others) started to realize the benefits of promoting women, recognizing what women bring to organizations: a new perspective, a range of ideas, and a broad skill set. However, when we did our research five years ago, we found that the women who were especially successful didn't rely solely on organizational initiatives. They also credited themselves (and the help and insights of other senior women and men) for their success: their tenacity, skills, and competencies. Indeed, one of the major findings of our research was that senior women's success was an effective combination of organizational and individual strategies.

Now, in the early part of the twenty-first century, we see the next stage in success not only for women but for women and men throughout their careers. As I stated in the introduction, one of the comments we frequently hear from major organizations is that despite numerous initiatives and programs and support from senior management, they still don't see the widespread, organizationwide results that they would have predicted five to ten years ago. Why not? Lynn and I believe that the next step in the evolution of career—and personal—success is an effective partnership between employees, especially women, and their organizations. However, in our opinion there is now a far greater need on the part of the employee, either a woman or a man, to take responsibility for one's career and personal development. We're hearing that from our clients, as well: "We want our employees to take charge of their careers and become more accountable."

We have spoken to thousands of women and men about this in the last several years, and the common theme has become, "Okay, you have the tools—or at least access to the tool box. What are you going to do with it?"

We need to take a far more proactive role in our careers. I truly believe that ten years ago most women thought that it was the organization's responsibility to help them become successful, and to some degree it was. But now it's time to move on. Is there still organizational responsibility? Of course. That's never going to change. But once an environment is established in which success can be achieved, it is our responsibility to make it happen—proactively, not reactively!

One thing that surprised me as a professional woman was how much I learned during this project. I can't tell you how many times I would listen to the insights of successful men and women during interviews and enthusiastically say to myself, "Yes, yes, this is fantastic; this is exactly what we all need to hear!" and "Wow, I wish I had heard this information ten or fifteen years ago, when I was starting my career." Lynn and I said exactly the same thing. Is it too late? Absolutely not. One of the reasons I included many quotes in each chapter was to underscore the importance of these issues. For me, it takes me a few times hearing the same feedback or observation before I finally think, Hey, I think there's a good message here.

Take the message. Zero in on what will work for you. Don't get overwhelmed with a lot of details that don't pertain to you anymore, the stuff that you already know. But make sure that you share this with the next generation. You tend to forget what it was like when you were in their shoes.

In conclusion, I hope that you have gained some of the same insights I did from these unbelievably talented people. I hope that you were able to see yourself in some of the stories. Most of all, I hope you enjoyed it. Keep up the good work. Maybe next time we'll be calling you for an interview.

Endnotes

Chapter 1: Develop Your Personal Brand: Acquiring and Promoting Key Competencies and Skills

1. Tom Peters, "The Brand Called You," *Fast Company,* August 1997, p. 83.
2. Ibid.
3. Anna Muoio, "Women and Men, Work and Power," *Fast Company,* February 1998, p. 71.

Chapter 2: Create an Image and a Style That Work for You

1. Tom Peters, "Leadership is Confusing as Hell," *Fast Company Online,* March 2001, p. 124.
2. Kathleen Jamieson Hall, *Beyond the Double Bind: Women and Leadership,* Oxford University Press, New York, 1997, p. 129.
3. Anna Muoio, "Women and Men, Work and Power," *Fast Company,* February 1998, p. 71.
4. Ibid.
5. Jerry Useem, "A Manager for All Seasons," *Fortune Online,* April 30, 2001.
6. Adrienne Mendel, *How Men Think,* Fawcett Columbine, New York, 1996, p. 41.

Chapter 3: Define Your Role as a Team Leader or Participant

1. Keith Hammonds, "Grassroots Leadership: U.S. Military Academy," *Fast Company,* June 2001, p. 106.

2. Russ Mitchell, "How to Manage Geeks," *Fast Company*, June 1999, p. 174.

3. Jerry Useem, "Leadership: What It Takes," *Fortune Online*, November 12, 2001.

4. Ibid.

5. Gary Klein, "Why Won't They Follow Simple Directions?" *Across the Board*, February 2000, pp. 15–19.

6. Jennifer McFarland, "Leading Quietly," *Harvard Management Update*, July 2001, pp. 3–4.

7. Tom Peters, "The Brand Called You," *Fast Company*, August 1997, p. 83.

8. Betsy Wiesendanger, "To Grow Your Company, Leverage Your Leaders," *Fast Company*, February 2001, p. 68.

9. Eric Matson, "She Picks the Projects That Work," *Fast Company*, December 1997, p. 196.

10. "How to Lead When You're Not the Boss," *Harvard Management Update*, March 2000, pp. 3–4.

11. Martin Gargiuio, "Informal Networks, Social Control and Third Party Cooperation," *INSEAD Knowledge Online*, August 2001.

12. Alan Webber, "Are You a Star at Work?" *Fast Company*, June 1998, p. 114.

Chapter 4: Develop a Mentoring Network

1. Kathy Kram, *Mentoring at Work: Developmental Relationships in Organizational Life*, University Press of America, Lanham, MD, 1988, pp. 84–87.

2. David Foote, "Leaders Are Made, Not Born," *Computerworld Online*, March 12, 2001.

3. Jennifer McFarland, "Leading Quietly," *Harvard Management Update*, July 2001, pp. 3–4.

4. Lloyd G. Trotter, "GE Mentoring Program Turns Underlings into Teachers of the Web," *Wall Street Journal*, February 15, 2000, p. B1.

Chapter 5: Build Effective Networks

1. Alan Webber, "Are You a Star at Work?" *Fast Company*, June 1998, p. 114.

2. Anna Muoio, "Women and Men, Work and Power," *Fast Company*, February 1998, p. 71.

3. Cheskin Research & Santa Clara University, Women Entrepreneurs Study, January 2000.

4. Tom Peters, "Leadership Is Confusing As Hell," *Fast Company*, March 2001, p. 82.

5. Peter York, "Super-Marketable You," *Management Today*, August 1999, p. 83.

6. Cheryl Dahle, "Xtreme Teams," *Fast Company*, November 1999, p. 31.

7. Linda Tischler, "Extreme Networking: MBAs Show the Way," *Fast Company Online*, July 2001.

8. Ibid.

9. Carol Hymowitz, "Managing Your Career," *Wall Street Journal*, November 6, 2001, p. B1.

Chapter 6: Gain Global Experience and Insights

1. "International Experience and Financial Performance," *Wharton Leadership Digest Online*, April 2000.

2. Leadership in the Global Economy—2000 Survey, *Watson Wyatt Advantage Online*, March 2001.

3. "International Experience and Financial Performance," *Wharton Leadership Digest Online*, April 2000.

4. "Survey of Top 50 CEOs," *Worth*, May 2001.

5. Vijay Govindarajan and Anil Gupta, "Building an Effective Global Business Team," *MIT Sloan Management Review Online*, Summer 2001.

6. Timothy R. Kayworth et al., "Leadership Effectiveness in Global Virtual Teams," *INSEAD Knowledge Online*, August 2001.

7. "CEO Study: Chief Executives in the New Europe," Association of Executive Search Consultants Europe, November 1998.

8. "The Power 50," *National Post* 2001 Annual Report.

9. Ibid.

10. PriceWaterhouse Coopers and the World Economic Forum, 2000 Survey on International CEOs and Technology.

11. "The Power 50," *National Post* 2001 Annual Report.

12. 2001 Regional Survey, *Hewitt Asia Quarterly.*

13. "The CEO Challenge 2001: Top Marketplace and Management Issues," The Conference Board.

Chapter 7: Take Charge of Your Own Career

1. Polly LaBarre, "Marcus Buckingham Thinks Your Boss Has an Attitude Problem," *Fast Company,* August 2001, p. 88.

Chapter 8: Develop Winning Communication Skills

1. Anna Muoio, "Women and Men, Work and Power," *Fast Company,* February 1998, p. 71.

2. Alan Webber, "Are You a Star at Work?" *Fast Company,* June 1998, p. 114.

3. "Letter from the Founding Editors: Leadership 2.0," *Fast Company Online,* June 1998, p. 16.

4. John Joseph, "Leadership Under Threat: Consult and Communicate," *Wharton Leadership Digest Online,* September 2001.

Chapter 9: Develop Key Leadership Skills

1. Paul Thornton, "Three C's of Leadership," *CEO Refresher Online,* August 2001.

2. Ruth Williams and Joseph Cothrel, "Tomorrow's Leaders Today," *Strategy and Leadership,* September to October 1997, p. 49.

3. "Letter from the Founding Editors: Leadership 2.0," *Fast Company Online,* June 1999.

4. Staff Article, "Decide Now!" *Management Today,* July 1999, p. 58.

5. CEO Profile, BristolMyersSquibb.com homepage.

6. Staff Article, *Assessment Matters Journal Online,* March 2001.

7. Staff Article, "Decide Now!" *Management Today,* July 1999, p. 58.

8. Ruth Williams and Joseph Cothrel, "Tomorrow's Leaders Today," *Strategy and Leadership,* September–October 1997, p. 49.

9. "Trend Watch," *Training & Development,* November 2000, p. 17.

10. Anni Layne, "How the President Leads," *Fast Company Online,* November 2000.

11. Graduate Management Admission Council, 2001 Survey.

Chapter 10: Develop the Next Generation of Leaders

1. Jennifer McFarland, "Leading Quietly," Harvard Management Update, July 2001, pp. 3–4.

2. Debra Meyerson, *Tempered Radicals: How People Use Differences to Inspire Change at Work,* Harvard Business School Press, Cambridge, MA, September 2001, p. 166.

3. Tom Peters, "Leadership Is Confusing As Hell," *Fast Company,* March 2001, p. 82.

4. "Grow Your Own Managers," *Sales and Marketing Management,* December 2000, pp. 87–92.

5. Debra Meyerson, *Tempered Radicals: How People Use Differences to Inspire Change at Work,* Harvard Business School Press, Cambridge, MA, September 2001, p. 166.

6. Russ Mitchell, "How to Manage Geeks," *Fast Company,* June 1999, p. 174.

7. D. Quinn Mills, *E-Leadership: Guiding Your Business to Success in the New Economy,* Prentice Hall Press, New York, 2001, p. 138.

8. "CEO Awakenings," *CEOgo.com,* August 2001.

9. Ibid.

10. Betsy Wiesendanger, "To Grow Your Company, Leverage Your Leaders," *Fast Company,* February 2001, p. 68.

11. "Designing Women: A Qualitative Study of the Glass Ceiling for Women in Technology," *SAM Advanced Management Journal Online,* Spring 2001.

12. Claire Raines, *The Xers and the Boomers: From Adversaries to Allies,* Crisp Trade Books, Menlo Park, CA, 1997, p. 48.

13. Bruce Tulgan, *Managing Generation X: How to Bring Out the Best in Young Talent,* W.W. Norton, New York, 2000, p. 40.

14. "Career Column Survey," *Fortune,* March 16, 1998, p. 167.

15. "Survival Kit for Project Managers," *Fast Company Online,* June 14, 2001.

16. Ram Charan, "Three Career Junctions Where Managers Need Help," *Business 2.0 Online,* May 9, 2001.

Index

About the Authors

Dr. Donna Brooks has conducted extensive research on the changes in organizational culture, with her findings reported to the U.S. Department of Labor. Having received her doctorate in organizational development, she is a frequent speaker for Fortune 500 corporations, major universities, and political forums. Dr. Brooks has also served on the Wharton Export Network Panel at the University of Pennsylvania's Wharton School and as the U.S. Executive Vice-President of the European Women's Management Development Network, based in Brussels, Belgium. She is currently a managing partner in Brooks Consulting, an international training and consulting firm.

Her twin sister, Lynn, has fifteen years of experience in international sales and marketing with several multinational corporations. Currently a partner at Brooks Consulting, Lynn also holds a stockbroker's license, as well as a B.A. in French and an M.A. in education.

Lynn and Donna have lived, worked, and traveled abroad—in Europe, Asia/Pacific, Latin America, and Africa. Both authors attended universities in France and Italy—Donna is conversant in four languages, while Lynn has found good use for her training in seven languages. The Brooks twins have also been invited to attend the prestigious "Renaissance Weekend." In addition to their busy work and travel schedules, Donna and Lynn have also completely renovated three houses.

Following the publication of their first book, *Seven Secrets of Successful Women* (McGraw-Hill, 1997, paperback release, 1999), Donna and Lynn were interviewed by *Working Woman, Fast Company, Cosmopolitan,* and *Marie Claire* magazines, *USA Today, The Chicago Tribune,* CNBC, Fox, NBC, CBS, NPR, iVillage.com, *NEWS* magazine (Austria), *Recruit* magazine (Hong Kong) and numerous other media in the United States and abroad.

To date, their book has been translated into eight languages: German, Spanish, Japanese, Portuguese, Dutch, Chinese (two dialects), and Thai. The publication was also featured as Amazon.com's Business Editor's Book Choice of the Month and Women.com's Book of the Month.

Their clients include American Express, Arthur Andersen, AT&T, Bell Atlantic/Nynex, Citigroup/Saloman Smith Barney, CS First Boston, DuPont, Ingersoll-Rand, Janssen Pharmaceutica, Johnson & Johnson, Johnson & Johnson Health Care, KPMG, Lucent, Marriott, Merck, Merrill Lynch, Morgan, Lewis & Bockius, National Association of Women Legislators, Ortho Biotech, Pfizer, Price Waterhouse Coopers, Rohm & Haas, TIAA-Cref, UBS Warburg, Unisys, Verizon, and Wyeth Ayerst.